He Who Dwells

Finding Our True Home in Christ

He Who Dwells

Finding Our True Home
in Christ

Bob Cofield

gatekeeper press
Columbus, Ohio

He Who Dwells: Finding Our True Home in Christ

Published by Gatekeeper Press
2167 Stringtown Rd, Suite 109
Columbus, OH 43123-2989
www.GatekeeperPress.com

Library of Congress Control Number: 2021933074
ISBN (paperback): 9781662910487
eISBN: 9781662910494

"He who dwells in the shelter of the Most High
Will abide in the shadow of the Almighty." *(Psalms 91:1)*

This book is dedicated to my incredible wife of 38 years, Sara, who has with patience and love been the living embodiment of Proverbs 31 for me, learning with me through that time to dwell in Christ as we have walked together. I would also like to thank my friends and brothers in Christ, Dutch Holland, Johnny Crain and Pastor Rick Oglesby, and my own pastors Joel Frederick and Johnye Horton, of Grace Life Baptist Church, each of whom gave me their prayers, encouragement and advice at a crucial time.

An image often repeated in Scripture is that of dwelling under God's protective wings:

He who dwells in the shelter of the Most High
Will abide in the shadow of the Almighty....

He will cover you with His pinions [wing feathers],
And under His wings you may seek refuge;
His faithfulness is a shield and bulwark....

For you have made the Lord, my refuge,
Even the Most High, **your dwelling place.** *(Psalms 91:1, 4, 9)*

Let me **dwell** *in Your tent forever;*
Let me take refuge in the shelter of Your wings. *Selah. (Psalms 61:4)*

Jerusalem, Jerusalem, who kills the prophets and stones those who are sent to her! **How often I wanted to gather your children together, the way a hen gathers her chicks under her wings,** *and you were unwilling. (Matthew 23:37)*

Table of Contents

Introduction

Wait...what? This entire book is about **dwelling?** I mean, shouldn't we all be more concerned about **doing** something or **going** somewhere? Answer: The deepest longing of our souls is to **dwell** with Christ, and we may not even realize it yet. **We were designed to dwell, to find our true home in Him,** and we can't even really begin to "go and tell" anyone until we have first dwelt with our Savior, or else we would have nothing to tell when we arrived. Dwelling with Christ is not mundane; it is life-changing. It is not passive inactivity; although, it does involve finding true rest for our souls, as we shall see. Neither is it simply acquiring intellectual knowledge about God; although, having that knowledge from Scripture is essential. It was, rather, God's major purpose all along in creating mankind—to have us **dwell** with Him in an intimate and life-changing relationship.[1] In fact, the Scriptures tell us that we were "chosen in Christ before the foundation of the world" and "created for good works which God prepared before-hand that we should walk in them" (Ephesians 1:4, 2:10). That's incredible love and dedication on God's part, as reflected in the image of His Son, Jesus Christ, being on the cross,

---

[1] See II Corinthians 6:16, Revelation 21:3 and Ezekiel 37:27 for just a few places where God states this.

1

suffering on our behalf "according to the kind intention of His will" towards us (Ephesians 1:5).

Much as Christ spread His arms in love for us on the cross, another image of that same love, purpose and dedication that we find repeated several times in Scripture is one of fledgling eaglets dwelling in their nest under the spread, protective wings of their parents. This is the image reflected in the cover art and also in the Scriptural epigraphs at the beginning of this book. There are several video clips on the Internet of mother eagles doing just that while in their nests, being almost completely covered with snow![2] The mother eagle in her nest is just one of many such pictures that the Scriptures present to us, reflecting God's incredible purpose to have us dwell with Him. There are others. The (Samaritan) woman at the well in John 4, for example, had a brief encounter with Jesus before going and telling an entire city to come and see their long-expected Messiah. "Come see a man who has told me all the things I have done; this could not be the Christ, could it?" But think about what happened in just those few moments she spent dwelling with Jesus before going. In her few moments with Him, He concisely explored with her His mission on Earth, the deepest secrets of her personal life, her deepest spiritual longings (using one of the most beautiful metaphors in all of Scripture, that of "living water"), and the coming Church Age in the eschatological (End Times) plan for the Kingdom of God. In short, He changed the entire direction of her life and set her upon a life-long quest for greater intimacy with Himself. So, what could

---

[2] In this case, the eggs were yet to be hatched. See for example https://www.youtube.com/watch?v=AOsdsxcgiEA. The actual nests can be up to ten feet in diameter, requiring up to three months to construct, and the adult eagle's wingspan can be up to seven feet! The younger eaglets start out as mere nondescript fuzzballs before they mature enough to make their initial flights, often from over 100 feet in elevation.

happen between us and Christ if we were to regularly and intentionally practice dwelling with Him, and welcome Him and cooperate with Him as He dwells in us? Another lesson from this event in John 4 is that the time to start dwelling is always the present. It is, very much, a come-as-you-are (although, not **remain**-as-you-are) affair. Just come in repentance, surrender and belief, and He will take it from there!

This book is about what God—the sovereign, almighty, eternal, loving, holy, triune God of the Bible—has done for us, to enable us to be reconciled with Himself, to know Him as a shield, refuge, counselor, and comforter, and even to have intimate fellowship with Him. I offer this to you not in any sense as one who has mastered the practice of dwelling in Christ, but rather as one who is amazed and aware that He (God) is actively dwelling in me. As a fellow follower of Jesus Christ, these are more or less my "field notes" documenting what I have learned and am continuing to learn from my life experience, from the Scriptures, and from various commentaries, teachers and other authors, as this all relates to Christ dwelling in me and me dwelling in Him. In fact, as I will share in more detail below, there was a time in my own walk with Christ when I became very discouraged, to the point of giving up; so, I can readily identify with those of you who may have been through (or are currently going through) similar experiences. In **Chapter 1.4**, "A Personal Note on Dwelling," I explore in more detail my own experiences in this regard, but here's the point that needs to be emphasized here: **There remains hope for any who truly seek Him.** As the Scriptures say, "A bruised reed He will not break / And a dimly burning wick He will not extinguish..." (Isaiah 42:3). **That means He is actively, even tenderly, in the rescue and restore business—thank goodness!** He is always there to meet us at our deepest points of failure and need, and He is able to forgive and to understand our deepest frustrations, discouragements and disappointments. Please allow this incredible fact to soak in: He was, and remains to this day, completely human Himself (yet without sin)![3] So, what about our lives will He not be able to completely understand? Having said all this, I realize that this book will remain offensive to some if it is to be true to the teachings of Scripture because Jesus could be "a stone of stumbling and a rock of offense; for they stumble because they are [actively, unrepentantly] disobedient to the word..." (I Peter 2:7-8). If you find yourself in that category, please don't put this book down just yet, and also please don't despair—it could all change for the better in just an instant.

Many people believe that, if there is a God, He is remote and out-of-touch with the daily affairs of mankind (a belief system known as Deism). The Bible says in Psalms 139, however, that God is "intimately acquainted with all of our ways" and is actually right this minute eagerly searching our hearts to determine our needs: "Before there is a word on our tongue, He does know it all."[4] Also, as we find in Psalms 31, He "has known the troubles of [our] soul[s]." Psalms 56:8 adds that He "keeps all of our tears in [His] bottle and records them in [His] book" and He has "taken account of all our wanderings." He (Christ) is continually before the

---

[3] Although, please note, He is also completely God and is now in a glorified body at the right hand of the Father. The Holy Spirit, as the third Person of the Trinity, also completely God, is now with believers at all times. I believe the Bible teaches that if we have one Person of the Trinity, we have Them all. Please refer to John 14:9, "If you have seen me , you have seen the Father," John 10:30—"I and the Father are one," John 14:16—"I will ask the Father, and He will give you another Helper, that He may be with you forever," and John 16:7—"But I tell you the truth, it is to your advantage that I go away; for if I do not go away, the Helper will not come to you; but if I go, I will send Him to you."

[4] This Psalm is, perhaps, the greatest statement of God's omniscience and omnipresence in the entire Bible.

throne of His Father interceding on our behalf (Romans 8:34). In the End Times (again, according to the Bible), after God has incinerated and then recreated the entire heavens and the earth (II Peter 3:10-12, and more will be said in what follows about the veracity, accuracy and reliability of Scripture[5]), and the New Jerusalem descends out of heaven upon the new earth, "made ready as a bride adorned for her husband" (Revelation 21:2), then a voice from the throne will say, "Behold, the tabernacle of God is among men, and He will *dwell* among them, and they will be His people, and God Himself will be [**dwelling**] among them" (Revelation 21:3). I would submit to you that will have been His goal all along—*to* *dwell* among *His people*. It's what men and women were created for in Genesis 2. It was the purpose of the tabernacle (a word meaning 'temporary dwelling place of God' in Hebrew[6]), and of the pillar of fire by night and cloud by day while they were in the desert, and later of the temple. It was the purpose of "the Word becoming flesh and dwelling among us" (John 1:14), and it remains His purpose today as He indwells believers in the person of His Holy Spirit as "earnest money," or a down payment, for the time when He will dwell with us once again, face-to-face. That's being anything but remote!

So, I invite you, if you are already a believer in and follower of Jesus Christ, to imagine the possibilities: finding greater peace, meaning and purpose in daily life, and knowing more intimately our Creator as Comforter, Counselor and Refuge. Or, if you have not yet taken that initial step of repentance and faith, I invite you to ask yourself the following: "Just what if it actually turns out to

---

[5] An excellent resource on this topic is Robert Plummer's book *40 Questions About Interpreting the Bible (40 Questions and Answers Series)*, by Robert L. Plummer and Benjamin Merkle (Grand Rapids, MI: Kregel Publications, 2010).
[6] "Moreover, I will make My **dwelling** among you, and My soul will not reject you" (Leviticus 26:11).

all be true? What would I stand to gain, and what could I finally be able to put away—fear, guilt, shame, anxiety, loneliness?" Could your current concept of God have possibly been shaped by disappointment or a bad experience with others who identified themselves as Christians? Why not make the effort to examine the original source again to see if you have the full, correct picture? What does this God have to say of Himself? After answering this question, my plan is to next thoroughly explore what it means to dwell, and how it is possible to do this amidst a fallen world increasingly hostile toward the Christian faith. Dwelling must refer to something greater than simply coexisting with Him, or what would be the point of making such a big deal over it (the word *dwell* is used well over 250 times in the Bible)? In formal theology this topic is referred to as "The Doctrine of Union with Christ." Our purpose here is simply to explore that doctrine from a layperson's perspective. [7] Having done this, we will move on to examine twelve other key spiritual edicts (for our purposes, eight of these are in bold letters to indicate they may be considered core edicts), all from Scripture and all largely synonymous with dwelling. In addition, all are themselves intransitive verbs (that means they designate actions we must take upon ourselves): **abide, wait**, watch, **pray**, fast, **worship, rest, study, meditate**, sit, **walk** and stand.[8] Our God makes some incredible promises for those who practice these. Special attention will be given to the

---

[7] Wayne Grudem's *Systematic Theology* devotes ten pages to discussion of this topic, which may all be summarized in Galatians 2:20 (see this verse quoted in **Chapter 1**). It became my life verse, as I describe, in 1991. See Grudem, Wayne, "Union with Christ" Chapter 43, *Systematic Theology* (Leicester England: Intervarsity Press, 1994), pages 840-850. This topic is also at the heart of what is currently being referred to by theologians as "Spiritual Formation." It is addressed in such books as *The Divine Conspiracy* (1997) and *Renovation of the Heart* (2002) by Dallas Willard.

[8] This list is not exhaustive. The commands listed were selected on the basis of their congruence with the concept of dwelling.

distinction in meaning and usage between these words, as for example the distinction between *abide* and *dwell.* I hope it will become evident by the time we conclude that our **dwelling** with God—recognizing, enjoying, reflecting on, and acknowledging His glory, and offering Him the **worship** He deserves—was His purpose in the creation of mankind all along.

In this book I have taken a pre-millennial perspective on the End Times.[9] I find it relevant to the topic of dwelling to explore such matters because it will be in the End Times that our Lord will consummate all He has done and has promised to do to enable us to dwell with Him and be His people. I know of many godly men and women who surpass me in intelligence, ability and dedication to our LORD, who hold either an a-millennial or a post-millennial perspective, and I would never break fellowship with any of them over this difference in views. I can only put onto these pages, however, what I interpret the Bible to say in its plain sense (where use of figurative language is not intended by the author, of course).

I have used a good many Scripture references in writing this book, making a deliberate attempt to base what I say about having a relationship with God upon God's own words, sharing my own experiences only where I felt it was appropriate to do so. However, in reading this book, readers may want to pass over many of these Scriptural references, pausing only when I have quoted the entire referenced passage in the text or when readers have a particular interest in investigating the Biblical source on the point being discussed. In this book I have also used the convention of putting words and phrases that need emphasis in boldface instead of italics, because I feel they will be more readily noticed within their contexts. Where quotations from Scripture contain such key

---

[9] You can refer to **Appendix 4** to find out exactly what that means.

words as *dwell, abide, wait, pray, worship, rest, study, meditate* or *walk,* the emphasis added is my own. This is done particularly in Parts II and III. Italics are used with book titles, epigraphs, foreign words, words used as the words themselves (as above with the words *dwell* and *abide*), within quotations from other sources that themselves employ italics, and from Scripture where the NASB itself uses italics (usually meaning that the words were implied in the original languages). A forward slash mark (/) indicates a line break in quoted Scriptures that are in poetic form. Finally, this book contains more than its fair share of footnotes; however, this need not be a distraction for readers of electronic versions. It should be possible to press and hold the footnote number with your finger to get an image of the complete footnote, without having to leave the page! Also, titles of chapters, sections and appendices in the Table of Contents are linked to their beginning pages in the text.

On now to Part I, where we consider how God as the Initiator always makes the first move to dwell in us, so we can then respond and reciprocate by dwelling in Him and making Him our true Home (at first a seeming paradox).

Part I

Dwell—First He in Us, Then We in Him

Chapter 1

First, He in Us

Or do you not know that your body is a temple of the Holy Spirit who is in you, whom you have from God, and that you are not your own? (I Corinthians 6:19)

1.1 Longing and Dwelling

As I have aged, I have found myself needing to get up from bed during the night more frequently. It is often during these times that I am acutely aware of my longing for God, and over the years, some of the sweetest times I have enjoyed in His presence and in His Word have been in the middle of the night. I have found that David had similar experiences, as he recorded them for us in the Psalms he wrote (which are, actually, the equivalent of his prayer journal entries, but more will be said about that in **Chapter 4**). Psalms 63 was written during a time when David had fled into the wilderness from his enemies. Here, in the quiet and alone with his thoughts, he expresses his longing for God:

O God, You are my God; I shall seek You earnestly;
My soul thirsts for You, my flesh yearns for You,
In a dry and weary land where there is no water....

When I remember You on my bed,
I meditate on You in the night watches,
For You have been my help,
And in the shadow of Your wings I sing for joy.
My soul clings to You;
Your right hand upholds me. (Psalms 63:1, 6-7)

According to His own words, you and I were created to *dwell* with God, in His very presence (in Latin that's *Coram Deo*), both now and for eternity. He is currently engaged in bringing that to pass.

For thus says the high and exalted One
Who lives forever, whose name is Holy,
"I **dwell** on a high and holy place
And also **with the contrite and lowly of spirit**
In order to revive the spirit of the lowly
And to revive the heart of the contrite. (Isaiah 57:15)

Jesus told his disciples before He went to the cross and then ascended into heaven, "If I go and prepare a place for you, I will come again and receive you to Myself, **that where I am,** *there* **you may be also**" (John 14:3). In praying to His Father He said, "Father, I desire that they also, whom You have given Me, **be with Me where I am,** so that they may see My glory which You have given Me, for You loved Me before the foundation of the world." In fact, whether we realize it yet or not, *dwelling* with Him is the deepest longing of our souls. Brent Curtis and John Eldredge identify this longing most eloquently in their book *The Sacred Romance*:

Some years into our spiritual journey, after the waves of anticipation that mark the beginning of any pilgrimage have begun to ebb into life's middle years of service and busyness, a voice speaks to us in the midst of all we are doing. *There is something missing in all of this*, it suggests. *There is something more...You long to be in a love affair, an adventure. You were made for something more. You know it....* This longing is the most powerful part of any human personality. It fuels our search for meaning, for wholeness, for a sense of being truly alive. However we may describe this deep desire, it is the most important thing about us, our heart of hearts, the passion of our life. And the voice that calls to us in this place is none other than the voice of God.[10]

Continuing along that same line of thought, James 4:5 says,

Or do you think that the Scripture speaks to no purpose: "He jealously desires the Spirit which He has made to dwell in us"?

Psalms 84 is likely a "Psalms of Ascents" written by some gatekeepers of the temple. That means that it was recited by the Israelites as they walked "up" to Jerusalem to celebrate the feasts ordained by God (often through some desolate and dangerous places—the Valley of Baca in verse 6, for instance). These were the walking public worshipers.[11] The temple was, effectively, the dwelling place of their God (specifically, His Shekinah[12] glory

---

[10] Curtis, Brent and John Eldredge. *The Sacred Romance*. Nashville: Thomas Nelson Publishers, 1997. 1,2,7.

[11] I first heard this phrase used by Harry Walls at Shades Mountain Independent Church, August 2007. It should really also describe us as NT believers—see the discussion in **Chapter 7** on the command to walk.

[12] This word is not actually found in the Bible, but is from the Talmudic writings, which were basically elaborations and commentaries on God's law. It is of interest here because its root meaning is God's *dwelling* place. Our Holy

resided behind a veil and between the tips of the Cherubim's wings in the Holy of Holies on the lid of the Ark of the Covenant [known as the "Mercy Seat"], and the High Priest could enter there only once each year to sprinkle blood in atonement for sin—a picture of Christ's atoning sacrifice for us). The temple, and its predecessor the tabernacle, were constructed in a pattern of concentric circles around God's presence. As one advanced from the outside wall to the Holy of Holies, that person would be subject to increasingly greater restrictions put in place to protect God's holy presence. What is of interest here is the passionate desire of the Israelite worshipers to be as close as possible to God's presence. They could dwell in the Promised Land, but they could not enjoy the intimate, personal dwelling that we are now able to enjoy in Christ on this side of the cross.

Psalms 84:1-2, 4, 5, 10 tells us:

> How lovely are Your **dwelling places** O LORD of hosts!
> My soul longed and even yearned for the **courts** of the LORD.
> My heart and my flesh sing for joy to the living God....
> How blessed are those who **dwell** in your **house**!
> They are ever praising you....
> How blessed is the man whose strength is in You,
> In whose heart are the highways of Zion! ...
> For a day in your **courts** is better than a thousand outside.
> I would rather stand at the threshold of the **house** of my God
> than **dwell** in the tents of wickedness.

Here's the great news—the veil of that temple (the "courts" or "house" the psalmist is longing for) that separated the priests from the "Holy of Holies" was torn completely in two at the crucifixion

---

God was going to great effort here to make a way to dwell among His sinful people.

of Christ! We may now enter freely and dwell with Him continuously! No more passing through concentric circles of increasing restriction or arduous pilgrimage is necessary. We only need to "confess our sins" (I John 1:9) to restore broken fellowship and return to dwelling. The highway image in the above passage carries two important ideas: (1) God is One Who reverses impossible situations, turning deserts into gardens and highways, for example; and (2) that highway, or way back to God, is now internal for us,[13] and as Brent Curtis and John Eldredge point out above, **we are all internally hardwired to undertake the journey of returning home.** "How blessed is the man whose strength is in you, in whose heart are the highways to Zion!" (Psalms 84:5, above).

So, our deepest longing is to dwell in and with Him, and His consuming passion is to dwell in and with us. Now, if dwelling with God doesn't sound exciting enough to you, then your concept of Him may be inaccurate. David was dwelling in Him when he faced Goliath. The Puritan pilgrims were dwelling in Him as they endured hardships, crossing the uncharted waters of the Atlantic to found Plymouth Colony. Tim Tebow was dwelling in Him as he won the Heisman Trophy. Joni Ericson Tada has dwelt in Him from a wheelchair for almost 50 years as a quadriplegic, giving hope and encouragement to multitudes. And countless Christian martyrs in countries where Christianity is forbidden have given, and continue giving, their lives while dwelling in Christ. Let's face it, He (God) is Who He is ("I am Who I am" [Exodus 3:14]), whether we ever come to accept and admit that to ourselves or not (and the Bible teaches us that someday we all

---

[13] This is not to say that we merely "look into our own hearts" to find God (an idea advanced in much contemporary thought about spirituality). We are not God; we are His creation, and He indwells us when we allow Him to do so through faith in His Word.

shall). That means that a great number of people will be greatly, even tragically, surprised or disappointed after they die to discover just Who God actually is.[14] Just think of some of the things He has created out of nothing (*ex nihilo*) and currently "holds together" (Hebrews 1:2-3, Colossians 1:15-23): the human brain and hand, the unimaginably vast reaches of the universe (countless stars, black holes and supernovae), the mind-boggling principles of quantum physics,[15] Class V whitewater rapids, mountains, double black diamond ski slopes, tigers, whales, delicate micro-organisms and DNA molecules, beagle puppies, you name it.

As I write this, a new black hole has been discovered with a mass seventy times greater than our sun. Stunned scientists claim it should not even exist in our galaxy. If our universe is expanding,

---

[14] At this point, I should mention "Pascal's Wager." A seventeenth-century mathematician, physicist and philosopher, Blaise Pascal postulated that, considering the two possible outcomes, it would be wiser to at least be open to the possibility that the God of the Bible does in fact exist. That may be a starting point, but it does not in itself constitute saving faith. In fact, the Bible states that no one may come to Christ unless the Father draws that person (John 6:44). An excellent book for those who are in doubt concerning God's existence is Richard E. Simmons III's *Reflections on the Existence of God* (Birmingham, AL: Union Hill Publishing, 2019).

[15] Currently, the hot topics in quantum physics seem to be (judging from my Twitter and Google feeds) whether (1) quantum computers may be developed, (2) there is such a thing as absolute reality at all, and (3) time travel is possible. I personally believe I could make the case Biblically that only God is outside the limitations of time and space; that scientists will discover a new law consistent with the laws of classical physics, existing at an even deeper level to account for the fact that reality seems to know whether or not or it has been observed, and to fix its identity accordingly; and that Christ will return before He allows humans to manipulate anything violating the classical laws of physics (as they are currently stated), enabling them to time-travel. A good book to read on this general topic is *The Creator and the Cosmos* by Hugh Ross. Also, Francis Schaeffer's book *Escape from Reason* outlines the history of intellectual thought concerning what is real and true.

as science says it is, then what lies beyond the frontier of its expansion? We can only imagine. God has left us in a universe that is so vast, varied and complex that we could devote our lifetimes (as many have) to trying to understand it better and never know all its secrets. When the Biblical character Job questioned God's greatness, goodness and wisdom, God asked him a long series of questions about His work of creation that each began with something like, "Okay, if you think you know so much, then please tell me—where were you when I created..." (Job 38:1-42:6). Again, according to His own words, we ourselves were originally created in God's image, including our own imagination, creativity, ability to reason, and ability to acquire knowledge (Genesis 1:26). That means that your wildest dreams and imaginings could ultimately owe their existence to God; so, boring? No, not in the least! And why then should we expect dwelling with Him in eternity would be anything less spectacular? "In my Father's house are many dwelling places" (John 14:2). I don't have any Scripture to directly back this up (except perhaps I Corinthians 2:6[16] and Ephesians 2:10[17]), but it seems to be consistent with all else I do know about Him. I believe that the "many (different?) dwelling places" in eternity that He refers to will be individually tailored to match the way He created us as individuals.[18]

1.2 The One Qualification for Dwelling with God

Who may dwell with God? This is simple, but it may surprise you. The answer is found explicitly in Psalms 15, Micah 6:8, Psalms 31

---

[16] "...what no eye has seen nor ear heard, nor the heart of man conceived, God has prepared for those who love Him."

[17] "For we are His workmanship [literally, poem or masterpiece work of art] created in Christ for good works which God prepared beforehand that we should walk in them."

[18] Randy Alcorn explores this and similar ideas in his book *Heaven*.

and Psalms 27:4-6; in a word, that one who has **integrity** may dwell. Now, we must preface any discussion of possessing integrity and dwelling with God with the understanding from Isaiah 64:6[19] and Romans 3:10-12 that "there is no one who is righteous." How, then, might we possess integrity if none of us is righteous? The answer lies in the word *imputation*, a term describing how the very righteousness of Christ is "reckoned" or credited to "our account" (to put it in accounting terms) when we place our trust in His sacrificial death to satisfy or propitiate, in a legal sense, God's demands.[20] Romans 3 and 4 are elaborations of this concept. **Appendix 9** is a detailed, graphical explanation of the gospel (plan of salvation). The Scriptures are clear that sin has initially separated all of us from God (Isaiah 59:2), and when we put our trust in Christ's sacrificial death on the cross, He is able to "bring

---

[19] The text says that "all of our righteousness is like filthy rags." If you're interested, try doing a word study on *"filthy rags."* It will dispel any notion you might have that the God of the Bible will be impressed enough with your works to allow you to dwell in His holy presence.

[20] Our pastor identifies **"Four Great Transfers"** that take place in the Bible, with respect to salvation (Joel Frederick, March 8, 2020, Grace Life Baptist Church): **(1)** Adam's sin transferred to us (Psalms 51:5): "Behold, I was brought forth in iniquity, / And in sin my mother conceived me." **(2)** Our sin transferred to Christ on the cross, in a legal sense (Colossians 2:13-14): "When you were dead in your transgressions and the uncircumcision of your flesh, He made you alive together with Him, having forgiven us all our transgressions, having canceled out the certificate of debt consisting of [legal] decrees against us, which was hostile to us; and He has taken it out of the way, having nailed it to the cross." (Isaiah 53:12): "...Yet He Himself bore the sin of many, and interceded for the transgressors." **(3)** Christ's righteousness transferred to us (II Corinthians 5:21): "He made Him who knew no sin to be sin on our behalf, so that we might become the righteousness of God in Him." **(4)** Our bodies resurrected, transformed and reunited with our souls at the Rapture (I Thessalonians 4:16): "For the Lord Himself will descend from heaven with a shout, with the voice of the Archangel and with the trumpet of God, and the dead in Christ will rise first." See **Appendix 9** for a detailed, graphical explanation how we can be saved to begin dwelling with God.

us to God" (I Peter 3:18). We are then able to **dwell** with God because Christ's righteousness has been imputed to us. This transaction requires integrity on our part.

Integrity means more than just honesty. It is the idea of moral and spiritual wholeness or soundness, of being undivided in soul or intention. If a storm were to pass through this area with flooding, engineers might be dispatched to determine if a particular bridge maintained its structural integrity (i.e., was sound in all its parts). One compromised part could cause the entire bridge to collapse. So, the opposite of integrity is not simply dishonesty; it is what the Bible calls double-mindedness, or having a divided or double heart (embracing opposite or opposing views—both good and evil—at the same time, or trying to have two Gods at the same time, the true one and a false one). A double-minded person would not be "sound in all of his or her parts." James writes, "...purify your hearts, you double-minded..." (James 4:8). James 1:8, I Chronicles 12:33 and Psalms 12:2 also speak of this, as does Psalms 86:11: "Teach me Your way, O Lord; / I will walk in Your truth; / **Unite my heart** to fear Your name." Integrity, on the other hand, is to will one thing.[21] It is being "single-minded." It is a

---

[21] As I understand the terms, *double-mindedness* should not be confused with *duplicity*, a similar but, in the main, distinctly different concept. Duplicity is having a hidden (most often evil) agenda, and trying to conceal that fact from others and to deceive them about it in the process. It is the same concept behind our term *two-faced*. In essence it means showing a false face to others, as with a mask, while maintaining a different heart behind the mask. On the other hand, a double-minded person may be honest about his or her internal struggle with conflicting desires or idols, in which case that person could be struggling against double-mindedness but not be duplicitous. In addition, having conflicting desires does not in itself make a person double-minded, but attempting to embrace and accommodate those conflicting desires does. Every one of us will continue struggling to completely put to death our sinful natures until we see Christ face-to-face, but for someone to willingly make provision for

returning to the heart and mindset that we have when Christ's righteousness is initially imputed to us, as in, "Hey, LORD, I'm all-in with You. Search my heart…try me…" (Psalms 139:1, 23-24). Psalms 32:2 says, "How blessed is the man to whom the Lord does not impute iniquity, / **And in whose spirit there is no deceit!**"

There used to be a popular tract entitled "My Heart Christ's Home."[22] Christ enters the home and seeks to visit each area ("room") of our lives, until He comes to the very places we want most to hide from Him. This idea of holding something back is seen in the story of the rich young ruler coming to Jesus to ask what he must do to obtain eternal life.[23] He apparently thought he might add eternal life to the list of things he owned and that his heart was devoted to. After telling Jesus that he had kept all of the commandments, Jesus put His finger on **the "one thing"** the man lacked: "Go and sell all that you have and give to the poor, and then come and follow me!" (Luke 18:18-25, my paraphrase). That **one thing** is everything to this particular man; and the man, unwilling to do as Jesus asks, goes away empty-handed, possessing everything but what matters most. It may be something other than

the flesh, while attempting to remain in fellowship with Christ, indicates double-mindedness. As was said earlier, **dwelling with Christ requires integrity** or whole-heartedness, even as we may continue to struggle. It is a choice we must continually make, and it will necessarily involve repentance. As quoted below, Psalms 32:2 says, "How blessed is the man in whose spirit there is no deceit." This psalm is thought to have been from David after he had sinned with Bathsheba and Uriah, her husband, and Nathan the prophet had confronted him about his sin. He goes on to describe his misery while he "kept silent about [his] sin." Coming clean, as with I John 1:9, is the answer. Thank goodness He rescues, forgives and restores!

[22] "My Heart Christ's Home" by Robert Boyd Munger, originally published by Intervarsity Christian Fellowship in 1954, 43rd printing, 1977.

[23] I got the idea for this illustration from an essay appearing in *World Magazine* by Janie B. Cheaney entitled "The One Thing," dated 9 May 2020, p. 20.

riches for someone else—anything that could take the first place in our lives ahead of God. **That highlights what it means to dwell with Christ—holding nothing back. Being all-in. Settling down and being at home with Him (the literal meaning of this word *dwell* in the Greek[24]).** Now, this is something we do in initially coming to Christ,[25] but it has to be regularly realigned whenever we get off-track, and for most of us that's pretty much daily. That's a life-long process called sanctification.[26]

I John 1:9 says, "If we confess our sins, He is faithful and just and will forgive our sins and cleanse us from all unrighteousness." The great paradox in the Christian faith is that we must first die before we are able to truly live. Paul tells us in Galatians 2:20 that he has been "crucified with Christ" and Luke records Jesus' words in Luke 9:23, telling us, "If anyone would come after me, let him deny himself and take up his cross daily and follow me. For whoever desires to save his life will lose it, but whoever loses his life for my sake will save it" (my paraphrase). The cross was an instrument of death. He calls us to die (be crucified) initially in coming to Him, then again daily to take up our own crosses as we follow Him through the life-long sanctification process. Here, again we encounter this concept of **integrity**. Salvation is an all-or-nothing, being-all-in affair. We cannot be partially alive and partially dead at the same time. We cannot be double-minded in coming to Him initially; neither can we maintain double-mindedness if we are to truly follow after Him. As martyred missionary Jim Elliot famously said, "He is no fool who gives what he cannot keep to gain that which he cannot lose." This has everything to do with

---

[24] Refer to **Appendix 1** for more detail.

[25] **Appendix 9**, "Understanding the Gospel," is a detailed graphical explanation of the gospel (the "good news" about how salvation is being made available in Christ).

[26] This concept is explained in more detail in **Appendix 9**.

dwelling in Christ. **Appendix 9** is a graphical explanation of the process of salvation, as both an initial step and also a life-long process of growing in Christ-likeness, culminating in our glorification following physical death (or The Rapture). Throughout this entire process God is the initiator through His Holy Spirit to convict us of sin and of our need for Him. We then respond in repentance and faith. First, He in us, then we in Him. Before we leave this important topic of integrity, please allow the following Scriptures to speak to your heart:

> O Lord, who may **abide** in Your tent?
> Who may **dwell** on your hill?
> He who walks with **integrity** and works righteousness,
> And **speaks truth in his heart**. (Psalms 15:1-2)

Question: How is "speaking the truth in one's heart" related to **integrity** and double-mindedness? To dwelling in Christ? David said in Psalms 51:6 (after being confronted over his sin with Bathsheba and in his confession), "Behold, You desire **truth in the innermost being**, and in the hidden part You will make me know wisdom." What is going on right now in my own "hidden part?"

> **One thing** I have asked from the LORD, that I shall seek:
> That I may **dwell** in the house of the LORD all the days of my life,
> And to meditate in His temple.
> For in the day of trouble He will conceal me in His tabernacle;
> In the secret place of His tent He will hide me;
> He will lift me up on a rock....
> When You said **"Seek my face,"** **my heart** said to You,
> **"Your face, O LORD, I shall seek."** (Psalms 27:4-5, 8)

<u>Question</u>: What is my "one thing?" Popularity? Success? Respect? Adulation? Self-fulfillment? What does it mean to seek God's face? Am I doing that now? What does that imply about the focus of my heart, desires and affections? David's one thing was to dwell in close fellowship with God. What sacrifices would such a thing require on my part?

Psalms 24:3-4 provides further insight:

> **Who may ascend into the holy hill of the LORD?**
> **And who may stand in His holy place?**
> He who has **clean hands and a pure heart,**
> Who has **not lifted up his soul to falsehood**
> And has **not sworn deceitfully.**
> He shall receive a blessing from the LORD
> And righteousness from the God of His salvation.

<u>Question</u>: What is this if not integrity? The **Holy hill** is the temple in Jerusalem, i.e., God's presence. Note his covering by the righteousness from the God of his salvation. Note, also, the **integrity** of the one who has a **pure heart and has not lifted up his soul to falsehood nor been deceitful.** No double-mindedness here!

The idea found in Psalms 27 above is to seek God in the integrity of our hearts in the place He may be found. The temple was the one place where God's presence was manifested in Old Testament times. For us today, **we** are God's temple (I Corinthians 3:16 and 3:19), if we have become true followers of Christ; so, we seek Him by cooperating with and becoming attentive to God's Spirit as He speaks to us through His Word. It is important to distinguish that we are not to seek God simply by looking within ourselves or by listening to our own fallen imaginations (as with the currently popular "contemplative or centering prayer"). Jerimiah 17:9 says that our hearts are "deceitful above all else and desperately sick" when left to their own devices, unguided by God's Word. On the other hand, we are not to simply write off all intellectual and creative effort by those who have not been converted to belief in Christ. We have all been created in the image of God[27] and bear resonances of that image, however twisted they may have become. Romans 1 states that we also have the witness of creation itself, so we "are without excuse." The mistake that is made in so much of the spirituality of today is to worship the creation itself (as in neopaganism[28]), instead of the Creator. The creation should indeed inspire us, but in such a way as to acknowledge and worship its Creator. God is the ultimate Creator, and because we are created in His image, He is the ultimate source of all creativity we may find within ourselves.

1.3 Hindrances to Dwelling

The greatest hindrances to dwelling seem to all be things we can control: **idols, busyness, Biblical illiteracy, negativity and legalism.**[29] First, an idol is anything, good or bad in itself, that takes the place of God in our lives, or that steals some of the devotion and affection that rightfully belong to Him. **An idol is something that falsely promises a home for our souls, a home that only Christ can truly provide.** The greatest idol in our current culture is self-fulfillment.[30] It is the Holy Grail or *summum bonum* of current

---

[27] See Fazale Rana and Hugh Ross's book *Who Was Adam?* for a great explanation of what it means to be created in the image of God. (Colorado Springs: NAVPRESS, Reasons to Believe, 2005, p. 79.)

[28] More will be said about this when discussing meditation in **Chapter 6**.

[29] Also, refer to the table "Habits and Hindrances" in the "Questions for Further Thought" at the end of **Chapter 9**.

[30] Our pastor identifies **Four Root Idols: Power** (longing for influence, respect and recognition), **Control** (longing for everything to go according to my plan),

culture. Abraham Maslow, an American psychologist and philosopher, theorized that the highest need of every person is self-actualization. This became the foundation of modern education theory and psychotherapy. In reality, self-actualization is a mirage, a dog chasing its own tail—it can never be achieved apart from Christ, because we were designed and created to bring glory to God, and in doing so we find our greatest self-actualization and fulfillment. In fact, without Godly self-restraint in place, self-actualization can easily result in self-destruction, and there are many famous examples of this (with addictions of various types being primary on the list). On the other hand, there are many examples of how living a godly life can bring about great personal fulfillment. For instance, our love for Christ need never be a zero-sum game with our love for others. Actually, the more we love Christ, the more we are able to love others. More specifically, the more I love Christ, the more He will enable me to love my wife and "to give myself up for her as Christ did for the church" (as He has commanded in Ephesians 5), or to love my children, by pointing out to me their value and needs. In doing that I find great self-fulfillment. More will be said in **Chapter 6** about self-actualization (or self-fulfillment) being a false god, but we must realize here that God hates this idol in particular.

Comfort (longing for pleasure, safety and security), and **Approval** (longing to be accepted, admired or desired). [Joel Frederick, Grace Life Baptist Church, from his sermon entitled "Captivity: Part 2," 17 January 2021.] This was adapted from Tim Keller, particularly from Keller's book *Counterfeit Gods*, 4 October 2011. The reference I found to it attributed it to Keller, David Powlison and Dick Keyes, in an article posted by Eric Geiger, "Four Root Idols," 1 October 2013 <ericgeiger.com/2013/10/four-root-idols/>. I also found these Four Root Idols in Tim Keller's book (with Sam Shammas and John Lin), *Gospel in Life: Grace Changes Everything (Study Guide)* (Grand Rapids, MI: Zondervan and Redeemer City to City and Redeemer Presbyterian Church, 2010), page 44.

Earlier, in the Introduction, Deism was mentioned as being a growing belief system. Deism is the belief that, if there is a God, He is remote and out of touch with the world. More currently, "Moralistic, Therapeutic Deism" is a phrase originating in a 2005 book entitled *Soul Searching: The Religious and Spiritual Lives of American Teenagers* by the sociologist Christian Smith with Melinda Lundquist Denton.[31] Moralistic, Therapeutic Deism is a self-defeating belief system. Its central tenants are that God just wants us to be happy and to feel good about ourselves. God does not necessarily need to be sought after or involved, unless there's a serious problem. If we're left to fend for ourselves and make sense out of life the best we can on our own, then each individual is free to define what is good by what is in the (perceived) personal best interests of that individual. But we cannot then turn right around and expect everyone else to agree with our own personal beliefs, goals and standards. The purpose of existence in this belief system is self-actualization for each individual, which may sound good, but in reality, can only be reached when each individual is dwelling in true submission to the one supreme God who designed us. One cannot have true morality or true self-actualization without this God being in the picture, and He must also be a God who is intimately involved in the affairs of everyday life. One has only to read the titles on the current *New York Times* Best-Seller List for self-help books and ask, "If everyone had the personal philosophy reflected in that title, what kind of place would this world be?" (For example: *You Are A Bad Ass: How to Stop Doubting Your Greatness and Start Living an Awesome Life.*) The fact is that Western Civilization has thrived for all these many past centuries because it was built upon the commonly-held Judeo-Christian worldview. It appears we are now,

---

[31] See, also, Albert Mohler's *The Gathering Storm*. (Nashville: Fidelitas Corporation, Nelson Books, 2020), pages 123-124.

in this Post-Christian Era, coasting into moral chaos, anarchy, strife and conflict.

Beth Moore, in her wonderful study on the Book of Daniel, calls Isaiah 47:8a "The Babylonian Motto." This verse comes in an oracle against Babylon, and it perfectly captures the ethos/worldview of our postmodern world:

> Now, then, hear this, you sensual one [Babylon],
> Who dwells securely,
> Who says in your heart,
> **"I am, and there is no one besides me…"**

More will be said about Babylon being both a literal place and a system of thinking organized in rebellion against God, to appear once again in the End Times. Here it is condemned as both, and the irony of the statement is obvious—there is only One who could truly make such a statement, and that is the one true God alone. He is the great **I Am**, the only self-existent One and truly self-fulfilled One, and He has determined this to be His very name.

God had earlier stated in Isaiah 44:6, 8:

> "Thus says the Lord, the King of Israel and his Redeemer, the Lord of hosts:
>
> **'I am the first and I am the last,**
> **And there is no God besides Me….**
>
> Do not tremble and do not be afraid;
> Have I not long since announced *it* to you and declared *it*?
> And you are My witnesses.
> **Is there any God besides Me,**

Or is there any *other* Rock?
I know of none.'"

So, this Babylonian line of thinking is completely antithetical to the mindset of anyone wishing to dwell with the one true God. That person will be denying self and finding self-fulfillment in the very process![32] Again, this brings to mind the passage from Luke 9:23-24, referenced earlier above:

> And He was saying to *them* all, "If anyone wishes to come after Me, he must deny himself, and take up his cross daily and follow Me. For whoever wishes to save his life will lose it, but whoever loses his life for My sake, he is the one who will save it..."

Remember, Babylon was a place of captivity[33] and the Babylonian way of thinking can become, in the present day, a false home for our souls. We must not allow this idol of self-fulfillment to take us captive!

---

[32] It is important to note here that self-denial is not to be an end in itself, as we find it practiced in monasteries. I believe the Bible teaches us to deny ourselves at the direction of our LORD, through his Word, as it applies to specific details of our lives. From my own experience, this most frequently involves a call to serve other people in some way.

[33] Although the Scriptures are clear that the LORD, Himself, had delivered Israel into physical captivity in Babylon for a defined period of seventy years, He did not intend for Israel to dwell in captivity to the Babylonian way of thinking. The time spent in Babylon was to be a corrective to the error that Israel had fallen into before God had allowed the Babylonians to seize them. We are today in much the same situation—finding ourselves immersed in an increasingly pagan culture that has turned its back on God, we are not to adopt our culture's way of thinking, but instead we are to return to worshipping the true I Am.

Second, if there is one overwhelming characteristic of life in "digital Babylon," it is busyness. Frazzled, frantic and frenetic, "we go 'round the prickly pear at five o'clock in the morning."[34] Most often we are uncertain of the reasons why, except for some vague notion that we may be missing out if we don't. It is called "FOMO" in today's social media lingo, short for "fear of missing out." Who has time to seek God's face in His Word when the herd is moving in ten minutes?[35] Dallas Willard, an authority on "spiritual formation" and author of *The Divine Conspiracy*, is quoted as advising that we "must ruthlessly eliminate hurry [from our lives], for hurry is the great enemy of spiritual life in our world today."[36] Jesus gave us a great lesson on busyness in Luke 10, when he visited the home of His close friends Mary and Martha. Martha was busy ("distracted") with all her preparations, while her sister Mary dwelt at Jesus' feet. When Martha asked Jesus to admonish Mary, He kindly told her that Mary had chosen the "**one thing**" that was needful (Luke 10:42). He was telling her that busyness does not always equal godliness, not that it is in itself wrong—it simply needs to be kept in its proper place, under submission to God's perfect will for us at any given time. That lesson has an incredible application for the days in which we live. In

---

[34] From T.S. Elliot's poem "The Hollow Men." Also, the book *Crazy Busy* by Kevin DeYoung is especially helpful on this topic.

[35] I have written a creative, satirical piece attached as **Appendix 2** that attempts to capture this state of mind. The piece is about the negative aspects of being short-sighted or myopic in approaching life. While it is true that God wants us to live always with the hope and certainty of eternity in mind (I Peter 1:3-4, Philippians 3:20, Romans 15:13, Titus 3:13 and Romans 12:12), he does also command us to live in "day-tight increments" (Matthew 6:34); that is, to "let the day's own trouble be sufficient for the day." There is no contradiction here—we can do both.

[36] Cited by John Ortburg in a *Christianity Today* article entitled "Ruthlessly Eliminate Hurry," July 4, 2002. Accessed 29 September 2020 <https://www.christianitytoday.com/pastors/2002/july online only/cln20704.html>.

our times, many display their busyness as a badge of honor, confirming or validating their self-worth, when our worth is actually to be derived from God alone (Acts 17:28 says, "In Him we live and move and have our being"). We are, in fact, commanded in Colossians 3:23-24 "to work heartily, whatever our task, as serving the Lord;" but again, that is to be done as serving the Lord, always keeping Him first. Done that way, God honors our hard work. A great deal of the book of Proverbs speaks to that subject. More will be said in **Chapter 5** about the divinely ordained rhythm of work and rest. Related to busyness in our times as a major hindrance to dwelling in Christ are digital distractions. More will be said in **Chapter 6** (on Studying and Meditating) regarding digital distractions; but it should be mentioned here that, while technology can bring incredible blessings into our lives (particularly in the midst of a pandemic), it can also insidiously weave its way into areas of our lives that properly belong to God. For instance, what's the first thing I do when I wake up each morning—is it to check my phone for text messages and my laptop for email, or is it to open God's Word and pray? Also, which is more important to me—friends and likes on Facebook and followers on Twitter, or gaining God's approval? You may have noticed that there is an obvious connection here to what was said earlier about idols being a hindrance.

Third, another major hindrance to dwelling is simple illiteracy, apathy or tone deafness ("dull of hearing" as it says in Acts 28:25-31) towards Scripture. It is the type of illiteracy or apathy that thinks it already knows, has "already been there and done that," or cannot possibly learn anything from a book, a person or a sermon that is so clearly culturally outdated and out-of-touch with the latest fashions of thinking. As I get older, I find myself occasionally looking for items that are right in front of me—so easy to miss the obvious! Could many be missing Christ because they consider that they have already tried reading the Bible and found it to be boring, irrelevant or obscure in meaning? To begin with, Christianity is in essence not an "it" but a "He." "He" is able to speak to us through the pages of the Bible, when we know enough about its contents to comprehend what is being said, and are open to the Holy Spirit's illumination of the text. I frequently hear people talking about the Bible, or even see them carrying one around, who don't seem to have a clue about what's inside it, except perhaps for a few popular verses. For example, the most popularly quoted verse today seems to be Matthew 7:1: "Judge not lest you be judged." This is often used as an irrefutable, end-of-argument proof-text or rejoinder anytime anyone makes a claim that something could actually be wrong or immoral (unless it conforms to the new generation's prevailing "progressive," "woke," "spiritual" new orthodoxy[37]). When one examines the entire chapter of Matthew 7, however, it becomes abundantly clear that the speaker (Christ, Himself) is encouraging his listeners merely to make sure they themselves are not at fault before they make discerning judgments about others. How many followers of Christ could explain the meaning of a random passage taken from a text, for example, like Isaiah or Revelation? How many "Nones"[38] would denigrate or write off the Bible without having actually read or seriously studied it? The point is that those who wish to dwell in Christ must make a home for their souls in the Scriptures. They must become dedicated, life-long students of the Word, and learn to love God with all of their **minds**. They must grow to so love hearing the voice of their God in the pages of the Bible that they feel

---

[37] See "Christians: Culture Warts or Faithful Servants?" Dr. Peter Jones, TruthXchange.com. (This was originally a two-part series printed September 12 and October 9 of 2012.) Accessed 18 August 2020 <truthxchange.com/2012/09/culture-warts-or-faithful-servants-part-1/>.

[38] "None" is a category of religious preference selected by a growing percentage of Millennials and members of Generation Z, to indicate that they have no religious preference at all.

as if they would perish or fall into complete despair if that were denied to them.[39]

Fourth, negativity—having a complaining, pessimistic, ungrateful spirit, one that focuses too much on the problems at hand—will be a hindrance to dwelling. Philippians 4:8 says, "Finally, brethren, whatever is true, whatever is honorable, whatever is right, whatever is pure, whatever is lovely, whatever is of good repute, if there is any excellence and if anything worthy of praise, **dwell** on these things." And lest we think that we must through our own efforts corral our own minds into such modes of thinking, verses 6-7 tell us that, once we make the choice and request it of God, He will "guard [our] hearts and [our] minds in Christ Jesus." The problem with negativity is that it not only robs us of our *shalom* (peace and wholeness) in dwelling in Christ, but it also insidiously weaves its way into the fabric of the Body of Christ, and in the process results in disunity, discord and wounded spirits. I am reminded of Hebrews 12:15 here, which warns us, "See to it that no one comes short of the grace of God; that no root of bitterness springing up causes trouble, and by it many be defiled…". When some fellow believer sins against us or does something to offend us, instead of nursing our grievance in our own minds and hearts, the Biblical response is to (1) forgive the person who offended us and (2) pray, asking the LORD's guidance and submitting our wills to His, and only then (3) approach that person directly (as opposed to discussing the matter with others behind his or her back), following the protocol laid out in Matthew

---

[39] Suggestion: If you currently have no plan, begin in the "emotional gymnasium" of Psalms, then read the Gospel of John, or read a portion of each daily. **Chapter 6** that follows gives more ideas about how we should actively seek to dwell in God through spending time in the Scriptures and in meditation. Henrietta Myers' book *What the Bible is All About* is a very helpful resource to use with your reading. The *Moody Bible Commentary* is another great resource to have ready for answering any questions that arise as you read.

18:15-17. Paul gives some good advice here: "Be kind to one another, tender-hearted, forgiving each other, just as God in Christ also has forgiven you" (Ephesians 4:32). For another example, if it is a grievance against church policy or decisions made, go in humility to speak with the pastor, elder, deacon or teacher concerned, to offer constructive feedback and seek a resolution. We might also try, for example, putting ourselves into the pastor's shoes—imagining how difficult it would be to grow a church, care for each member (in our case over one thousand), maintain a thriving missionary effort, orchestrate a building campaign and relocation, and do all of this in the midst of a pandemic! The point is that we should seek reconciliation in a spirit of humility, love and understanding, instead of a spirit of bitterness, acrimony and accusation. James gives some good advice here:

> *This* you know, my beloved brethren. But everyone must be quick to hear, slow to speak *and* slow to anger; for the anger of man does not achieve the righteousness of God. (James 1:19-20)

If the problem is a grievance against the government, we are first to obey those in authority over us and then seek to change the laws or policies we disagree with, through a lawful and non-violent manner. Romans 13:1-2 tells us plainly,

> Every person is to be in subjection to the governing authorities. For there is no authority except from God, and those which exist are established by God. Therefore, whoever resists authority has opposed the ordinance of God; and they who have opposed will receive condemnation upon themselves.

When required by the government to do something that directly violates the Word of God, however, we have the examples of Daniel

33

and his Hebrew colleagues to instruct us. In Daniel 6, we find Daniel delivered from the lions' den after disobeying the law that forbade him to pray. Similarly, his three companions escaped death in a fiery furnace after refusing to bow down and worship the pagan king of Babylon (Daniel 3). In their case the pre-incarnate LORD, Himself, was seen standing with them in the flames! But in each case, the Hebrews maintained their general submission, deference and respect to the God-ordained authorities over them. The bottom line about negativity is that a Biblical response to our fleshly inclination to embrace negativity is to humble ourselves, fear God and seek reconciliation through His guidance. And one final thought: No Christian would dispute that we are commanded to praise God and to be thankful to Him. This would be impossible to do by anyone harboring a spirit of negativity!

Finally, legalism—the idea that we are compelled to unrelentingly practice certain disciplines or to obey certain rules in order to earn the privilege of dwelling with Christ—can be a major hindrance to actually dwelling with Him. This was the idea the Pharisees had, for which they were sternly rebuked by Jesus. "They tie up heavy burdens and lay them on men's shoulders, but they themselves are unwilling to move them with *so much as* a finger" (Matthew 23:4). Obeying God had become, for them, merely ostentatious and obsequious ritual and routine, while they had "neglected the weightier provisions of the law: justice and mercy and faithfulness; but these are the things [they] should have done without neglecting the others" (Matthew 23:23). **True dwelling with Christ is predicated upon neither ritual nor routine, but rather upon relationship**. I think of King David, a "man after God's own heart" (Acts 13:22), who failed so utterly to keep the Law by his sin with Bathsheba and later with her husband, Uriah, and even tried to sweep it all under the rug until Nathan the prophet came to confront him (in II Samuel 12).[40] Once confronted, however, David pours out his soul before God (recorded in Psalms 51 and 32) in repentance. That's how God brought David into restored fellowship with Himself. David asked God to

> Create in me a clean heart, O God,
> And renew a steadfast spirit within me.
> Do not cast me away from Your presence
> And do not take Your Holy Spirit from me.
> Restore to me the joy of Your salvation
> And sustain me with a willing spirit. (Psalms 51:10-12)

David didn't earn his way back into fellowship and dwelling with God. God is always more concerned with where our hearts are at any given time in our relationship with Him than He is with our lack of a legally perfect track record (which only Jesus had). As has often been said, "The heart of our problem is the problem of our hearts." More will be said in **Chapter 5** about avoiding the trap of legalism.

That, by the way, brings us to the main point that distinguishes Christianity from all other world religions. Other world religions have their lists of things one must do (or not do, as the case may be) in order to be good enough to dwell with God. Consequently, adherents of these other religious traditions must all live in varying degrees of dread and doom, with the awareness that they may have grossly failed to live up to this list of standards, or "fallen short" as it

---

[40] This is not even to mention David's failures as a parent, which ultimately led to his son Absalom's attempt to lead an armed insurrection against his father. More will be said about David's struggles with sin and his eventual victory over it in **Chapter 8**. I am so thankful that God included these examples of David and, later, the Apostle Paul in the Bible, because I myself am equally guilty of sin, and God accepted me back into His fellowship when I responded to Him in repentance, as I explain in more detail in the next section.

says in Romans 3:23. Christianity, on the other hand, also begins with its own list of things we have all failed to do, every one of us (Romans 3:23); **but** the purpose of this list is not to condemn us but to point out our need for Christ. Because He lived a sinless life as a perfect God-man, He was able to make a perfect sacrifice of His own life to settle our accounts with God. That frees us to then seek through His help to live according to His standards—His "list," if you will—out of gratitude, not out of dread or doom. What a huge difference! We are no longer bound by a legalistic mindset. We are bound by a "law of liberty" (and is that not an oxymoron to end all others?) to live as we were designed to live (James 1:25, 2:12). It's all based on His gift of grace! Legalism is therefore eliminated. Let us never return again to the line of thinking that says, "I must meet all of God's standards to be loved by Him, and I am accepted by Him on the basis of my own righteousness." I believe the Bible teaches that we may please Him with a righteous life, but we are unconditionally accepted by Him on the basis of His own righteous life. He therefore loves us now as much as He ever will.

So, to conclude: idols, busyness, illiteracy or apathy toward the Scriptures, negativity and legalism can all become hindrances in our dwelling with God. These are the "captors" vying to misdirect us from our true home in Christ.

1.4 A Personal Note on Dwelling

"Yes," you may be thinking at this point, "but how can I know this Bible you keep extolling is a reliable source of information about God?" Great question! I am now seventy-one years old. Forty-one years ago, I left my first career (in the military) to attend what I still believe to be the finest seminary in the world. Somehow chosen as president of my first-year class, I ended up actually losing my faith before that first year was over. I did! That was due, first and primarily, to the sin that was in my life at the time, and also to genuine unanswered questions and discouragements. I also had the mistaken notion ingrained in the back of my mind that the Christian life was mainly about a to-do list, as opposed to a relationship (dwelling) with the living God. So, back to "square one" for me. Very disorienting, painful and discouraging.

I believe some of you who are reading this may have undergone similar experiences, perhaps as young adults establishing your identities in a world now most often hostile toward Christian faith. Christian apologetics is the whole body of knowledge that addresses such questions as the reliability and veracity of the Scriptures, the reality of the Resurrection, the "Problem of Evil," etc., and there are currently numerous excellent evangelical apologetics organizations, books and other resources available for anyone who cares enough to dig for answers to the right questions.[41] Suffice it to say here that I spent the next several years undergoing God's discipline, reproof and correction (Hebrews 12:4-11), diligently reading about every religion I was aware of,

---

[41] An online search for "Evangelical Apologetics Resources" will yield helpful results. Two such websites are located at <seanmcdowell.org/blog/what-are-the-best-apologetics-resources-for-students> and <arcapologetics.org>. Another wonderful resource is a book by Robert L. Plummer (and Benjamin Merkle, Series Editor) entitled *40 Questions About Interpreting the Bible* (*40 Questions and Answers Series*) (Grand Rapids, MI: Kregel Publications, 2010). Additionally, Richard Simmons' excellent new book *Reflections on the Existence of God* (Birmingham: Union Hill Press, 2020) provides the most convincing arguments I have ever read for the existence of the God of the Bible. The book is part of a series of short, readable essays on the topic. Also, the books by Francis Schaeffer, Nancy Pearcey and Charles Colson are all very helpful in understanding how current thinking about the claims of the Bible has evolved through the centuries. James Sire's book, *The Universe Next Door*, is a "worldview catalog" contrasting Christianity with other worldviews. Finally, truthXchange is a ministry examining current cultural issues from an evangelical perspective <truthxchange.com>.

including Christianity, and conversing with and listening to a large number of people. J.D. Greear has said that God often does His best work in us when we are in difficulty, and when we wait upon Him for answers and deliverance, as found in Lamentations 3. I found that to be true in my own life. As I progressed, I actually compiled a developing outline of the things I could reaffirm as being my own personal beliefs. As G.K. Chesterton says in his book *Orthodoxy*, "I did try to found a little heresy of my own, and when I had put the last touches to it, I discovered it was orthodoxy."[42]

I first re-embraced monotheism, and then this one Father God I communicated with redirected me to the Christian gospel, which I had given up on, as His one and perfect way of bringing me into reconciliation with Himself. I then became reconvinced as to the reliability of the Bible, especially as contrasted with the sacred and foundational writings of other religions and belief systems. I cried out to this God of the Bible in repentance; and finally, feeling crushed and humbled, in "fear and trembling," as it says in Philippians 2:12, and in complete surrender and supplication for deliverance and answers. I came to realize after "wrestling with Him," much as Jacob had done in Genesis 32, that I simply could not improve on what He had done through the cross.[43] I did, however, come away from that struggle with my own "limp," as did Jacob (Genesis 32:22-32), and I did not get answers to all my

---

[42] Chesterton, G.K. *Orthodoxy: The Classic Account of a Remarkable Christian Experience*. Wheaton, IL: Harold Shaw Publishers, 1994. p. 7.

[43] In Genesis 28, after having a dream of "angels...ascending and descending on...a ladder [to] heaven," Jacob recognized that the place was "none other than the house of God" (God's dwelling place or a gate to heaven). He was fleeing a very dysfunctional family situation, an unlikely place for God to reaffirm His covenant with Jacob, based not upon Jacob's just desserts but God's covenantal faithfulness.

questions (Deuteronomy 29:29).[44] But on October 26, 1991, I took the Scripture memory card for Galatians 2:20 from the box of such cards I was keeping, and in complete repentance and surrender wrote the date on that card. I have not looked back since, except to wonder at the mercy, grace and patience of God.

I have been crucified with Christ. It is no longer I who live but Christ who lives in me, and the life I now live in the flesh I live by faith in the Son of God who loved me and gave Himself for me. (Galatians 2:20)

This verse, by the way, defines a way of transcendence through Christ (that is, getting beyond ourselves and our problems) that does not necessitate the abolition of desire, self, soul or individual identity, as do Eastern monistic approaches. Rather, these aspects of our personhood are redeemed, restored and enhanced in Christ. God met me as the father who runs to meet his prodigal son returning home in Luke 15. I am thankful beyond words that He so abundantly forgives, restores and redeems those who seek Him in repentance. I have come to realize that this well-known story in the Bible applies not only to our initial salvation, but also to any time in our Christian walk when we have turned away from Him in sin and rebellion. He always stands ready to accept us back when we repent and we are ready to obey Him. "Today, if you hear His voice, do not harden your hearts..." (Hebrews 3:15). He passionately wants to dwell with us, which brings us to our next topic as it concerns dwelling, His accessibility and approachability.

---

[44] Deuteronomy 29:29 says, "The secret things belong to the LORD our God, but the things revealed belong to us and to our children forever, that we may follow all the words of this law."

1.5 The Accessibility and Approachability of God through Christ for Penitent Believers

As I have been writing this book, I have been fortunate to come across another book that has been a tremendous encouragement for me: *Gentle and Lowly: The Heart of Christ for Sinners and Sufferers* by Dane Ortlund.[45] I have waited a very long time for such a book as this, and my wife and I read a chapter together each evening. What Ortlund has done, in a masterful way, is to reveal from Scripture what Christ has said of Himself, and what others have said of Him concerning His own heart. He has particularly drawn from the writings of several seventeenth-century Puritans, such as Richard Sibbes, Thomas Goodwin and John Bunyan, and from eighteenth-century theologian and pastor Jonathan Edwards. His "lodestar" text is Matthew 11:28-30, from which the book derives its title. This is "the only one place" in the entire Bible where "we hear Jesus open up to us His very own heart."[46] As we shall see later in **Chapter 5**, in this passage Jesus offers rest to all who would come to Him. He states that He is both gentle (meek, humble)—"the most understanding person in the universe….the posture most natural to Him is not a pointed finger but open arms,"—and lowly (humble)—"the meaning…overlaps with that of *gentle*, together creating a single reality about Jesus' heart."[47] "The point in saying that Jesus is lowly is that **He is accessible**…. For all His resplendent glory and dazzling holiness, His supreme uniqueness and otherness, no one in human history has ever been more approachable than Jesus Christ."[48] Two points made in this book stand out to me: (1) Jesus retained His complete humanity

---

[45] Dane Ortlund. *Gentle and Lowly: The Heart of Christ for Sinners and Sufferers* (Wheaton, IL: Crossway, 2020).
[46] Ibid., p. 18
[47] Ibid., p. 19
[48] Ibid., p. 20

through His resurrection and ascension, and is now as a result seated in heaven at the right hand of the Father, completely human (yet sinless) and completely God, and therefore completely able to understand and help us (Hebrews 2:18); and (2) Citing Puritan Thomas Goodwin and based on Hebrews 12:2, "Jesus Christ gets more joy and comfort than we do when we come to Him for help and mercy."[49] How could we not desire to dwell with such a Savior as this? How I needed to hear someone say that!

Ortlund also gives a helpful explanation of how each of the three Persons of the Triune Godhead are involved to provide what we need as we seek to dwell. The Spirit makes Christ's words to us real and personal (I Corinthians 2:12). He is our comforter, our counselor and our guide. He intercedes for us with "groanings too deep for words" (Romans 8:26). The Father is "the Father of mercies and the God of all comfort" (II Corinthians 1:3). He agreed with the Son in eternity past on Jesus' atoning sacrifice. He is, according to James 5:11, (much) compassionate. His righteous wrath against sin is more than matched by His compassion toward repentant sinners:

> A correct understanding of the triune God is not that of a Father whose central disposition is judgment and a Son whose central disposition is love. The heart of both is one and the same; this is, after all, one God, not two. Theirs is a heart of redeeming love, not compromising justice and wrath but beautifully satisfying justice and wrath.[50]

Jesus told Phillip in John 14:9-10, "Whoever has seen Me has seen the Father.... He [Jesus] is the tangible epitomization [sic] of God

---

[49] Ibid., p. 37
[50] Ibid., p. 131

[the Father]."[51] In the Scriptures the Father is pictured as a mother bird gathering His people under His wings (Psalms 61:4, 91:4 and 145:8-9). Affirming His preincarnate oneness with the Father, Jesus also used this image with convincing effect (speaking here before his triumphal entry into Jerusalem, leading up to his crucifixion):

> O Jerusalem, Jerusalem, *the city* that kills the prophets and stones those sent to her! How often I wanted to gather your children together, just as a hen *gathers* her brood under her wings, and you would not *have it!* (Luke 13:34)

Countless times the LORD both proclaimed and demonstrated His compassion toward His wayward people. I am reminded here of my wife's life verse, Lamentations 3:22-23:

> The Lord's [here referring to the Father's] lovingkindnesses indeed never cease,
> For His compassions never fail.
> *They* are new every morning;
> Great is Your faithfulness.

The Father is completely complicit in all that Christ is, does and has done for us (John 17:5, Ephesians 1:4 and Romans 8:28-30). The Son intercedes for us (Hebrews 7:25) as our Advocate (I John 2:1). He (Christ) stated that He is better able to do this now than He was during His earthly ministry (John 16:7) through the Spirit, Whom He sent to us after His ascension. So, all three persons of the Triune Godhead are intimately involved in our dwelling. Their accessibility and approachability draw us to dwell, and keep us there through all of life's discouragements, failures and setbacks.

---

[51] Ibid., p. 133

That brings us to think more about our part in dwelling, which is the subject of our next chapter.

To conclude this chapter, please allow me to quote a passage from Ortlund's book that highlights the amazing, ready compassion and acceptance God extends to those who seek to dwell with Him:

> God's heart of compassion confounds our intuitive predilections about how he loves to respond to his people if they would but dump in his lap the ruin and wreckage of their lives. He isn't like you. Even the most intense of human love is but the faintest echo of heaven's cascading abundance. His heartful thoughts for you outstrip what you can conceive. He intends to restore you into the radiant resplendence for which you were created. And that is dependent not on you keeping yourself clean but on you taking your mess to him. He doesn't limit himself to working with the unspoiled parts of us that remain after a lifetime of sinning. **His power runs so deep that he is able to redeem the very worst parts of our past into the most radiant parts of our future.** But we need to take those dark miseries to him [emphasis added].[52]

What an incomprehensibly wonderful God we have! He extends His love to us in a way that begs for our response. And what response does He require? Simply, come to Him all who labor and are heavy-laden!

> "For My thoughts are not your thoughts,
> Nor are your ways My ways," declares the Lord.
> "For *as* the heavens are higher than the earth,

---

[52] Ibid., Pages 160-161 Emphasis Added

So are My ways higher than your ways
And My thoughts than your thoughts." (Isaiah 55:8-9)

For thus says the high and exalted One
Who lives forever, whose name is Holy,
"I **dwell** *on* a high and holy place,
And *also* with the contrite and lowly of spirit
In order to revive the spirit of the lowly
And to revive the heart of the contrite. (Isaiah 57:15, repeated
from above)

1.6 For Further Thought

1. What does it mean for Christ to dwell in us? More will be said
    about this, and the seeming paradox that we also are to dwell
    in Him, in **Chapter 2**. Hint: God is always the initiator.

2. What is the one qualification for dwelling? What is my "one
    thing?"

3. What are the major hindrances to dwelling? Which of these
    seem most difficult to overcome? Can you think of others?

4. In being the initiator, how has God made Himself
    approachable and accessible to us, as sinners and sufferers?

5. How are each of the Persons of the Triune Godhead involved
    in enabling us to dwell?

Chapter 2

We in Him—More on Our Part in Dwelling in Christ

Let me dwell in Your tent forever / Let me take refuge in the shadow of Your wings. (Psalms 61:4)

In this chapter we will examine the seeming paradox of Christ dwelling in us while at the same time we are dwelling in Him. We will also ask and answer the question of why we need to dwell in Him in the first place—what exactly are we seeking refuge from when we seek to dwell in Him? Then we will examine what it means to trust God. This is relevant to the issue of dwelling in Christ, because dwelling implies that we are dependent upon Him for protection and sustenance; how may we know that He will provide these things that we need from Him? Finally, we will see how our dwelling in Him and His in us has been His plan all along from Creation until now and even into the future. First, now, to the seeming paradox.

2.1 A Seeming Paradox

A major aspect of understanding what it means to dwell is the seeming paradox that, while God is said to dwell in believers, believers are also commanded to dwell in Him,[53] to find our true home in Him. How can both occur at once? God's indwelling of believers in the person of the Holy Spirit (I Corinthians 3:16) occurs as a once-and-for-all event at the time of regeneration. We are said to have been sealed in Him (Ephesians 1:13). From that point forward, He will never leave us nor forsake us (Hebrews 13:5), although we can "grieve" Him (Ephesians 4:30). This is not to say the struggle ceases at the point of regeneration, only that we may then begin relying upon the ever-present Holy Spirit to keep us from falling (that's His part)—but we have to make that choice. Everyone continues to struggle (I John 1:9). From that point forward, we are commanded to daily "walk in the Spirit" (Ephesians 4:1-3, Luke 9:23), which is largely synonymous, as we shall see later in **Chapter 7**, with dwelling in Him. That's our part; but again, the Holy Spirit leads and enables us to do it. **There is a reciprocal relationship here.** So, in initiating, He dwells in us, and we in turn then dwell in Him as a response—at first, a seeming paradox. As Jesus says in John 14:20, "In that day you will know that I am in My Father, and **you in Me, and I in you.**"

Our pastor speaks often of having to "preach the gospel" to himself, and encourages us to do the same. By that, he means that he deliberately lets his faith inform his feelings, not the other way around. He reminds himself who Jesus is, what Jesus has done for

---

[53] The phrase *in Christ* is used 164 times in the Apostle Paul's letters, the Book of Ephesians primary among them, where it is used 75 times. This underscores the importance of the concept of being **in Christ** to dwelling and abiding. As our pastor has said, "**Our goal is not merely to move closer to Christ, but to dwell in Him, to abide in Him**" (Joel Frederick, Grace Life Baptist Church, 10 January 2021). More will be said about this in **Chapter 3**.

him and what He is doing for him right at that moment (praying for us—Hebrews 7:25). D. Martyn Lloyd-Jones, in his book *Spiritual Depression,* captures the same concept with his phrase "take [oneself] in-hand." This is the same concept expressed three times by the Psalmist in Psalms 42-43:

> Why are you in despair, oh my soul?
> And why have you become disturbed within me?
> Hope in God, for I shall again praise Him
> For the help of His presence. (Psalms 42:5)

This has everything to do with dwelling in Christ. Lloyd-Jones comments:

> You have to **take yourself in-hand**, you have to address yourself, preach to yourself, upbraid yourself, condemn yourself, exhort yourself, and say to yourself: 'Hope thou in God'—instead of muttering in this depressed, unhappy way. And then you must go on to remind yourself of God. Who God is, and what God is and what God has done, and what God has pledged Himself to do. Then having done that, end on this great note: defy yourself, and defy other people, and defy the devil and the whole world, and say with this man: 'I shall yet praise Him for the help of His countenance [the word *countenance* is *presence* in the NASB].'[54]

Paul David Tripp expresses this same idea beautifully, as only he can, in his book *New Morning Mercies: A Daily Gospel Devotional.* What he says is based on Psalms 42:

---

[54] Lloyd-Jones, D Martyn. *Spiritual Depression: Its Causes and Cure.* Grand Rapids, MI: Wm. B. Eerdmans Publishing Co., 1965. Page 21.

No one is more influential in your life than you are because no one talks to you more than you do. It's a fact that you and I are in an endless conversation with ourselves. Most of us have learned that it is best not to move our lips because people will think we're crazy, but we never stop talking to ourselves. In this inner discussion, we're always talking about God, life, others and ourselves, and the things we say to ourselves are very important because they are formative of the things we desire, choose, say and do. What have you been saying to you? What have you been saying to you about yourself? What have you been saying to you about God? What have you been saying to you about life, meaning and purpose, right and wrong, true and false and good and bad?... In Psalms 42 we're invited to eavesdrop on a man's private preaching.[55]

The more our thinking and talking to ourselves can be guided by God's Word, the better for us.

I have long struggled with depression. Perhaps some of you have experienced some of that also (as have an estimated 17.3 million adults in the United States[56]). That number has been predicted to increase, particularly among young people, in the days to come. Depression has been a major impediment for me in dwelling in Christ. I have found, however, that many of the Psalms, and other books of the Bible such as Lamentations and the prophets, contain urgent cries for deliverance from despair, and that it is possible for me to pour out my anxiety and sadness before God in honesty and to seek His deliverance. A major way I have learned to do this is

---

[55] Tripp, Paul David, *New Morning Mercies: A Daily Gospel Devotional.* (Wheaton, IL: Crossway, 2014), Entry for February 4.
[56]"Major Depression." National Institute of Mental Health. 7 January 2019, last updated February 2019. <https://www.nimh.gov>.

through journaling, which I can only describe as an extremely cathartic process. My journal entries most often directly address God, and I use His covenant name (translated as "I Am") in addressing Him, which in the NASB is designated as LORD (all upper-case letters)—because it reminds me of His essential lovingkindness toward those who belong to Him in a covenant relationship through Jesus' blood (see Lamentations 3:22-23). So, my journal becomes an extended prayer when I do this. Now, please tell me—what exactly is what I have just described, if not *dwelling*? What begins in anguish and despair for me can end in comfort, assurance and praise as I "take my soul in-hand" through the pages of my journal and His Word (I also write a great deal in my Bible). Dwelling is active, not passive. By the way, I would strongly recommend that you never digitize your journals if you keep them. A journal should be a place where one can explore his or her deepest anxieties, fears and longings with the LORD. So, the only place those things exist for me is on handwritten notebook sheets of paper. Journaling is a great way for me to think and pray because it helps me to clarify and focus my thoughts. Plus—and this gets more important as I grow older—it helps me to remember His acts of lovingkindness towards me, something of major importance to the LORD.

> "...when you pray, go into your inner room, close your door and pray to your Father who is in secret....and...do not use meaningless repetition." (Matthew 6:6-7)[57]

As mentioned earlier, that word *dwell*, or one of its derivatives (such as *dwelling or dwelling place*—either as a verb, noun or adjective), appears more than 250 times in the Bible, so it must be an important concept to God. At some point I began circling the

---

[57] More on prayer, as a facet of dwelling, comes in **Chapter 4**.

word as I came across it. My favorite reference/imagery is in Psalms 91:1-4, 9 (from which the title of this book is derived):

> "**He who dwells** in the **shelter** of the Most High
> Will **abide** in the **shadow** of the Almighty.
>
> [2] I will say to the Lord, "My **refuge and my fortress**,
> My God, in whom I trust!"
> [3] For it is He who delivers you from the snare of the **trapper**
> And from the deadly pestilence.
> [4] **He will cover you with His pinions** [wing feathers],
> **And under His wings you may seek refuge;**
> His faithfulness is **a shield and bulwark**....
>
> [9] For you have made the Lord, my **refuge**,
> *Even* the Most High, your **dwelling place**."

The same idea occurs again, in Psalms 61:4:

> Let me **dwell** in Your tent forever;
> Let me **take refuge in the shelter of Your wings**.

Does that not comfort you, give you optimism and hope, even the least bit? Or on the other hand, does it possibly make you feel somewhat uneasy? I would submit that your answer to that question may tell a great deal about how you currently stand in your relationship with God. To me, those are perhaps the most comforting words I have ever heard! In bold font above are the words and phrases that suggest an image of defenseless young eaglets under the protective wings of a parent. So, what do we need protection from, and why should we seek to find a refuge?

2.2 Dwelling in Exile Amidst a "Fallen," Often Hostile World

The believer is to "seek shelter in" or "find refuge in" God, which presents the obvious question: "What exactly are we needing to seek shelter and find refuge from?" Well, to begin with, the "world" actually hates us as followers of Christ because it first hated Christ. Speaking to His disciples, He said,

> If the world hates you, you know that it has hated Me before *it hated* you. If you were of the world, the world would love its own; but because you are not of the world, but I chose you out of the world, because of this the world hates you. Remember the word that I said to you, "A slave is not greater than his master." If they persecuted Me, they will also persecute you; if they kept My word, they will keep yours also. But all these things they will do to you for My name's sake, because they do not know the One who sent Me. If I had not come and spoken to them, they would not have sin, but now they have no excuse for their sin. He who hates Me hates My Father also. If I had not done among them the works which no one else did, they would not have sin; but now they have both seen and hated Me and My Father as well. But *they have done this* to fulfill the word that is written in their Law, "They hated Me without a cause." (John 15:18-25)

That is the main reason we need a place of refuge. **In fact, if you and I are not experiencing some blow-back or persecution for the stand we have taken for Christ (or we are not at least burdened by our concern for others who are), then we might legitimately question whether we are truly following (dwelling**

in) Him.[58] Once again, just listen to the words Jesus prayed for His disciples before his crucifixion:

> But now I come to You; and these things I speak in the world so that they may have My joy made full in themselves. I have given them Your word; and the world has hated them, because they are not of the world, even as I am not of the world. I do not ask You to take them out of the world, but to keep them from the evil *one*. They are not of the world, even as I am not of the world. Sanctify them in the truth; Your word is truth. As You sent Me into the world, I also have sent them into the world. For their sakes I sanctify Myself, that they themselves also may be sanctified in truth. (John 17:13-19)

The word *world* here (in Greek it's *cosmos*) is the whole system, or arrangement of thought, that is in opposition to God's thoughts. I John 2:15-16 informs us that the world is "the lust of the flesh, the lust of the eyes and the pride of life," which just happen to coincide with the three temptations Satan presented Jesus with while He was in the wilderness following His baptism, and the three temptations Eve faced in the Garden of Eden (Genesis 3:6). Make no mistake, we are all engaged in a great warfare. I Peter 5:8 says Satan "prowls around like a roaring lion seeking someone to devour," and Ephesians 6:12 says "our struggle is not against flesh and blood." Satan's objective is to steal, kill and destroy (John 10:10). When we dwell in Christ, we are safe from these threats. In addition, we live in a fallen world in which, "The best laid schemes o' mice an' men gang aft agley, / An' lea'e us nought but grief an'

---

[58]"Indeed, all who desire to live Godly lives in Christ Jesus will be persecuted" (II Timothy 3:12).

pain, / For promised joy!" as Robert Burns[59] says in his poem "To A Mouse, On Turning Her Up In Her Nest With a Plow." Often things just don't work out the way we think they ought to. We earn our living "by the sweat of our brow" amidst "thistles and thorns" (Genesis 3:17-19), a consequence of what is referred to as The Fall (the event that took place in the Garden of Eden, when sin was introduced[60]). "In the world you have tribulation," said Jesus, "but take courage; I have overcome the world" (John 16:33). One of the speakers in the Book of Job puts it like this: "...Man is born for trouble as the sparks fly upward" (Job 5:7).[61]

So, things can be tough for anyone trying to follow Christ in this fallen world as it stands now. As stated earlier, "Indeed, all who desire to live Godly lives in Christ Jesus will be persecuted" (II Timothy 3:12). In a very real sense, we may think of ourselves as being "in exile" here. We groan and creation groans, awaiting redemption (Romans 8:22-23). We are "strangers, aliens and exiles" here (I Peter 2:11), "poor, wayfaring strangers, 'a travelin' through this world of woe," as the old folk song goes. Another

---

[59] A famous Pre-Romantic poet from eighteenth-century Scotland. In modern English he says, "The best-laid schemes of mice and men often go astray and leave us nothing but grief and pain for promised joy." The title of the poem indicates that this very thing happened to the mouse.

[60] And if you have trouble with accepting the account in Genesis 3 as being anything beyond a myth, please just put that whole issue on mental hold for right now. Investigate the resources suggested above in **Chapter 1**, particularly the book by Robert Plummer, and ask yourself these questions: (1) When did I, personally, first rebel against what my heart-of-hearts told me was the will of God? (2) Why does evil exist in the world today? (3) Don't I recognize that there is something just fundamentally amiss ("messed-up," or as Burns says, "agley") with the way things are in this world today? **Appendix 8** is a poem I wrote on the idea of finding meaning amidst the fallenness of this world.

[61] The Second Law of Thermodynamics tells us the universe is tending towards disorganization (entropy) and energy must continuously be expended to maintain organization.

older song contains the lyrics, "This world is not my home, I'm just 'a passing through…and I can't feel at home in this world anymore."[62] That's true. This world is not our home! **Our true home is in Christ alone**—we are dwelling in Him while we are here in this fallen world temporarily, as if He were our "home away from home." As the lyrics to the old hymn go, "Blessed assurance, Jesus is mine. Oh, what a foretaste of glory divine!" That also reminds me of a nineteenth-century camp-meeting song (or chorus, actually) entitled "Camp A Little While in the Wilderness." The lyrics include the following: "We'll camp a little while in the wilderness. Then we'll all journey home." Almost seems as if the folks of yesteryear had a much better handle on this concept than we do today.

Philippians 3:20-21 says,

> For our citizenship is in heaven, from which also we eagerly wait for a Savior, the Lord Jesus Christ; who will transform the body of our humble state into conformity with the body of His glory, by the exertion of the power that He has even to subject all things to Himself.

We are between the "already" and the "not yet" aspects of our salvation.

> To live in the "now" and "not yet" of redemption is to **wait** on the Lord in all this activity's paradox-laden fulness—at once in process and already finished, groaning and joyful, spiritually painful and pleasurable. This is pilgrimage. This is

---

[62] Composed by J.R. Baxter (1887-1960). Public domain.

spiritual formation. This is a season of **waiting** that will end only when we die or Christ returns.[63]

More will be said on **waiting** in **Chapter 4**, and on the stages of redemption in **Appendix 9**, Part II.

In his book *The Church in Babylon*, Erwin Lutzer writes, "We've got to stop the Israel thinking, which is, 'this is our place, our home.' Instead, we must remember that we are foreigners and strangers in exile. **It's someone else's home. We're not in the Promised Land. If anything, we're in exile.**"[64] There was a period of seventy years in Israel's history, beginning in 586 BC, when the Southern Kingdom (all that was left after the Northern Kingdom had been carried into captivity by the Assyrians, never yet to return) was taken into captivity by the Babylonians, and Jerusalem was ravaged and the temple destroyed. This period is referred to by Bible students as The Exile.[65] The prophet Isaiah wrote during this period, predicting it as being God's corrective discipline. The prophet Jeremiah also wrote during this period and conveyed detailed instructions to the Israelites about how they should dwell while in captivity, and gave a firm promise regarding their restoration:

---

[63] Bradley Braun, *On Waiting Well: Moving from Endurance to Enjoyment When You're Waiting on God* (Chicago: Moody Publishers), p.125. Emphasis added.

[64] Lutzer, Erwin. *The Church in Babylon: Heeding the Call to Be a Light in the Darkness* (Chicago: Moody Publishers, 2018), p. 13, emphasis added. See also Ron Rhodes' new book *New Babylon Rising: The Emerging End Times World Order* (Eugene, OR: Harvest House Publishers, 2019).

[65] Not to be confused with the "Captivity" in Egypt, which lasted for 400 years, before the time of Moses. So, God's chosen people were well-acquainted with what it meant to be "strangers and exiles." To Moses God gave specific instructions about how the Israelites were to care for aliens in their midst.

"Seek the welfare of the city where I have sent you into exile, and pray to the Lord on its behalf, for in its welfare you will have welfare....When seventy years have been completed for Babylon, I will visit you and fulfill my good word for you, to bring you back to this place. For I know the plans I have for you," declares the LORD, "plans for welfare and not for calamity to give you a future and a hope.[66] Then you will call on Me and pray to Me, and I will listen to you. You will seek Me and find Me when you search for Me with all your heart. I will be found by you," declares the LORD, "and I will restore your fortunes and gather you from all the nations and from all the places where I have driven you," declares the LORD, "and I will bring you back to the place from where I sent you into exile.... Write all the words which I have spoken to you in a book. For behold, days are coming," declares the LORD, "when I will restore the fortunes of My people Israel and Judah."[67] The LORD says, "I will also bring them back to the land that I gave to their forefathers and they shall possess it." (Jerimiah 29:7-30:3[68])

Notice God intends for His people to be actively pursuing Him, even while we are in exile. He has sent us into a hostile world.

---

[66] Verse 11 is often taken as a specific promise to NT believers, when it is actually a promise to the OT Jews who were about to go into exile. It may be assumed, however, that the same God will deal with His people in the same way, whether OT or NT, and according to Ephesians 1:4 we are now His **chosen** people. This is not to say that the Church has replaced Israel in God's plan for the ages. It has not. More will be said about this in **Chapter 4** that follows. Also, **Appendices 3 and 4** are graphical explanations of how God will fulfill His promises to both the Church and Israel.

[67] And that's never been done...yet.

[68] And that's being done, even at the present time (since 1948).

We're not to develop a siege mentality,[69] but to engage our culture and to care for the needy around us. Knowing that we're only here temporarily, we are to "seek the welfare off the city where He has sent us" (verse 7). As we wait for His restoration and redemption, we are to be "salt and light" (Matthew 5:13-16). Christ's return is imminent (Matthew 24:42). At His return, the Bible teaches that He will establish an earthly kingdom for one thousand years, followed by new heavens and a new earth, where the New Jerusalem will be located (Revelation 20 and 21).[70] Jerusalem and Babylon, while being literal cities in both the Old Testament and the End Times, are also powerful symbols in Scripture for the places where God dwells (Jerusalem) and where Satan dwells (Babylon—pagan and anti-Christian). We are currently living in a world system dominated by Satan. We must be careful to distinguish here that, while God has allowed Satan temporary dominion, He (God) remains, ultimately, in absolute control even now as He "works all things after the counsel of His will" (Ephesians 1:11). Satan's complete defeat has already been decreed, but not yet enacted. Here's the point in all of this—it is within this milieu that we are called to dwell in Christ.

Randy Alcorn writes, "Why do God's children undergo pressures, suffering, and deadly peril? Paul answers clearly. 'That we might not rely on ourselves but on God' (II Corinthians 1:9, NIV). **There's no nearness to God without dependence on God**

---

[69] Admittedly, we must shield ourselves and our families from certain areas of our increasingly depraved culture while we work to transform that same culture. There is a fine line between seeking to understand the culture we are in so that we can work for its transformation, on the one hand, and devoting so much attention to it that it becomes acceptable to us, on the other. We must remember that we are but strangers and aliens, destined for a much better place, citizens of a much different kingdom.

[70] Refer to **Appendix 4** for an outline of events in this period.

[emphasis added]. And nothing makes us more dependent on Him than when the bottom drops out…. When we're feeling good, too often we rush on with too little thought of the God who is supposed to be our Rock and Sustainer and Comfort. He is our friend, and don't we always appreciate true friends most when we need them, in times of difficulty?"[71] **Dwelling in Him** is the Biblical prescription for such times, and difficulty is often God's prescribed method for drawing us to Himself. "For momentary, light affliction is producing for us an eternal weight of glory far beyond all comparison, while we look not at the things which are seen, but at the things which are not seen; for the things which are seen are temporal, but the things which are not seen are eternal" (II Corinthians 4:17-18). In a very real sense, we are like sheep in need of a Good Shepherd to protect and lead us (as Jesus describes in John 10) through a fallen and often dangerous world. One of my all-time favorite passages about how God understands the difficulties we face and the vexations our souls must endure (particularly as they involve conflicts with other people) in a fallen, hostile world is Psalms 31, a "lament psalm." This psalm assures us that He will provide Himself as a refuge, shelter and dwelling place:

> I will rejoice and be glad in Your lovingkindness,
> Because You have seen my affliction;
> You have known the troubles of my soul…
>
> How great is Your goodness,
> Which You have stored up for those who fear You,
> Which You have wrought for those who take refuge in You,
> Before the sons of men!
> You hide them in the secret place of Your presence from the

---

[71] Alcorn, Randy, "Discovering the Wonders of God in the Low Tides of Life," *Eternal Perspectives*, Summer/Spring 2020. pp. 4-5.

conspiracies of man;
You keep them secretly in a shelter from the strife of tongues.
(Psalms 31:7, 19-20)

The Navigator Wheel Illustration[72] beautifully summarizes the essential disciplines for one who seeks to dwell in Christ while in exile. The center of the wheel, as of the Christian life—where the power and direction are applied—is Christ, Himself, as LORD. The rim is the obedient Christian in action while being in the midst of a fallen, often hostile world. Christ's power and direction are transferred to the rim through the spokes which are the Word and prayer (vertical spokes) and fellowship and witnessing (horizontal spokes).[73] These disciplines will be present in the life of a follower of Christ because they are where Christ (through the Holy Spirit) will lead us. An important distinction must be made here, however, between having these disciplines out of love for and obedience to Christ, and attempting to use them to bring Christ into our lives or to earn His approval through practicing them. That type of effort would be fruitless, and could become insincere, done for the approval of others and for self-esteem, as with the Pharisees of Jesus' day. "When you pray, you shall not be as the hypocrites, for they love to stand and pray in the synagogues and in the corners of the streets, that they may be seen by men" (Matthew 6:5). When we seek to spend time with Christ for the right motives, it will gain the approval of God but it will not alter

---

[72] See <https://www.navigators.org/wp-content/uploads/2017/08/navtool-wheel.pdf>.

[73] The vertical spokes (prayer and God's Word) and the hub are the aspects of the Wheel illustration most directly related to dwelling, as you will see in Part II where we will discuss the eight other mandates for one seeking to dwell in Christ (including study, meditate and pray). The idea behind this diagram is that the vertical spokes concern our relationship with God, while the horizontal spokes concern our relationship with people.

His love for us, which is as complete for true followers of Christ now as it will ever be. By a conscious choice, we put Him into the center of our lives as LORD.[74] He will then build the disciplines of Word, prayer, fellowship and witnessing into our lives, as we obey him.

This simple but powerful diagram has had more impact upon my life,[75] and upon the lives of others, than I can describe. It was a verse used with this illustration (and the accompanying Navigator Topical Memory System) that became my "Life Verse," as I previously explained (Galatians 2:20). In a survey by the Barna Group it was found that over 51% of all church-going people in this country had never even heard of the Great Commission (Matthew 28:19-20)![76] It should be noted that this command by Christ was not, "Go and evangelize..." but rather "Go and make disciples... teaching them to observe all that I've commanded you." Big difference. That disciple-making process is identified most clearly in II Timothy 2:2, where Paul is speaking to his disciple Timothy: "The things which you have heard from me in the presence of many witnesses, entrust these to faithful men who will be able to teach others also." There is a significant amount of teaching involved here, by both word and example. Disciple-

---

[74] Again, referring to His covenant name, calling to mind His consistent, daily faithfulness to us (Lamentations 3:22-23).

[75] This was through the ministry of the Navigators while I was a college student and then for six years in the military following that. I am forever indebted to the men who poured their lives into mine, discipling me, and enabling me to pour my life into others, during that time!

[76] Source: Translating the Great Commission, Barna Group, 2018. Accessed 30 March 2021. <https://shop.barna.com/products/translating-the-great-commission?_pos=1&_sid=ccbcc2d60&_ss=r&utm_source=Newsletter&utm_medium=email&utm_content=Barna+Highlight%3A+A+surprising+response+to+%22The+Great+Commission%22&utm_campaign=2021-03-29_Highlight>.

making is therefore a life-to-life process, one only complete when the disciple who has been made is able to go then and reproduce his or her own faith-life in yet another person. There are four generations of disciples in this verse. Can you identify them? They are Paul, Timothy, faithful men and others also. That's the power of an exponential increase—the new disciples are themselves disciple-makers.[77] So, the total goes from one to two, then four, then eight, sixteen, thirty-two, sixty-four, etc. Our pastor has identified the presence of this process of disciple-making in the life of a follower of Christ as being a key indicator of how well that person is dwelling in Christ. So, these are the disciplines identified in this wheel illustration that should be found in our lives while we are in exile, in a world that is in many ways set against us. That seems to be challenge enough, does it not?

To be sure, however, our LORD will also at times allow illness, physical injury or even emotional pain to enter our lives. This is where we must distinguish true, Biblical doctrine from the "prosperity gospel" variety.[78] For every Peter who was delivered from prison when the disciples prayed, there is a Paul or a John

---

[77] There is a well-known illustration of the power in this process: Starting with one grain of wheat on the first square of a checkerboard and then doubling that on each succeeding square, one would have enough wheat on the final sixty-fourth square to equal about 2,000 times the world's annual production of wheat (1.4 trillion metric tons)! Complete that same process with disciples instead of with grains of wheat and that would then be more than enough disciples to easily evangelize and disciple the entire world! From Wikipedia, "Wheat and Chessboard Problem." Last updated 18 October 2020. Accessed 30 March 2021. <https://en.wikipedia.org/wiki/Wheat_and_chessboard_problem>.

[78] The typical response given by followers of such doctrine to not getting what we desired and asked for is that we just didn't have enough faith; so go back and try again! In such modes of thinking, it is possible that faith becomes its own object: they have faith in faith itself! This is not true Biblical faith, the object of which is God, Himself. Faith must have a valid object.

the Baptist who was martyred there; and for every Daniel who was delivered from the lions' den or Hebrew who was saved from the fiery furnace, there are multiple Christian martyrs who lost their lives to the lions in the Roman Coliseum. What we may always be sure of, however, is that (1) God is always in control and is in fact a "gate-keeper" over any harm that may befall us (reference Job's trials at the hands of Satan, Jesus' prayer in Gethsemane [John 22:42], and I Corinthians 10:13 where *temptation* may also mean *trial*), (2) He never forsakes us in the midst of trials (Hebrews 13:5), (3) He will always comfort us with a special measure of His grace to endure trials (witness the stoning of Stephen Acts 7:54-60), (4) that He cares deeply about our pain and loss (remember His weeping over Lazarus' death, which He deliberately allowed to occur by delaying His arrival), and (5) He will always redeem any suffering we endure for our good (Romans 8:28), His glory (John 9:3), our betterment (Hebrews 12:4-11), and our reward (Romans 12:3, James 1:12 and Revelation 2:10—the "crown of life"). Will we be found faithful? As Paul David Tripp has said,

> The fact is that you cannot make sense out of life unless you look at it from the vantage point of eternity. If all God's grace gives us is a little better here and now, if it doesn't finally fix all that sin had broken, then perhaps we have believed in vain: "If in Christ we have hope in this life only, we are of all people to be most pitied" (I Corinthians 15:19). There has to be more to God's plan than this world of sin, sickness, sorrow and death. There has to be more than the temporary pleasures of this physical world. Yes, there is more, and when you live like there is more to come, you live in a radically different way.[79]

---

[79] Tripp, Paul David. *New Morning Mercies: A Daily Devotional Guide* (Wheaton, IL: Crossway, 2014), entry for February 12.

Honestly, If Jesus' mission on this fallen earth had been to alleviate all suffering, then He failed dramatically.[80] This is not to say that He did not care deeply about **social injustice** (many of the Old Testament prophets preached passionately about it), **poverty** (recall in Luke 16:19-31 the story of the rich man and Lazarus), **hunger** (James 2:16 plus the feedings of the multitudes and the LORD's provision of manna in the wilderness), and the list continues. **I believe He will abolish all injustice when He returns and establishes His millennial kingdom (Revelation 20). In the interim, Christians are enjoined to be engaged in acts of charity and kindness, and to be loving each other and outsiders sacrificially (to "deny ourselves and take up our crosses daily to follow Him," Luke 9:23) in serving "the least of these." In this country, Christians and Christian organizations lead in efforts to care for and release people from poverty and injustice.** The remaining "mystery or 'problem' of evil" in the world, however, is this: why would a good/loving, omnipotent and omniscient God allow suffering to even exist to begin with? The answer I have come up with (and embraced as my own personal "theodicy"[81]) is one that runs from the story of "The Fall" in Genesis 3, to the Church Father Irenaeus, to the Romantic poet John Keats and then to the late theologian John Hick (with whom I have other major differences). It may be summarized with the following statement: This fallen world we live in is a "Vale of Soul-Making."[82] And to that I add that all misfortunes, confusion and

---

[80] And here's a verse that is difficult for many to reckon with: "Is it not from the mouth of the Most High that both good and ill go forth?" (Lamentations 3:38). Refer to the discussion that follows on "Trusting God" (2.3) for more on this topic.

[81] A theodicy is a formal explanation of "The Problem of Evil"—that is, if God is omnipotent and good, then why does He allow evil to exist in the world today?

[82] Here I feel as if I could write an entire book to elaborate, but just think about it like this: In Tolkien's *Lord of the Rings*, without Sauron and his One Ring and

chaos will someday make sense (I Corinthians 13:12, Isaiah 55:8-9 and Deuteronomy 29:29). I do, however, know enough right now of Jesus to know that He is the very definition of goodness, and I can completely trust Him with my life. In fact, He is the ultimate source of every good thing I have encountered in this life:

> Every good thing given and every perfect gift is from above, coming down from the Father of lights, with Whom there is no variation or shifting shadow. (James 1:17)

Before leaving our discussion of this important topic of social justice, I would be remiss if I did not at least mention the current major misunderstanding of this topic that is widespread within our culture, and has even gained a substantial foothold within the Church. As the term is currently used in secular society, *social justice* is not Biblical justice.[83] *Social Justice*, when used under the approach to social philosophy known as *Critical Race Theory*, is consumed with identifying "oppressor" groups and "oppressed" groups. Categories such as race, religious views, gender identity and sexual preference all "intersect" to define who is more oppressed and victimized than whom, and hence who has more moral authority to speak to the issues of social justice. Also, the Christian position on sin being the ultimate and universal problem, and Christ being the solution, is sometimes discredited. Since self-fulfillment and self-actualization are the ultimate goals of human existence for many in these aggrieved groups, any idea that certain behaviors may actually be sinful is rejected. The

---

Mordor (evil as a twisting or perversion of what is right, as elements of the narrative), what would Bilbo and Frodo ever have become? As it is, they rose to the occasion as heroes, through a vale of suffering.

[83] *Why Social Justice Is Not Biblical Justice,* by Scott David Allen (Grand Rapids, MI: Credo Communications, LLC, 2020) is an excellent resource on this subject.

ultimate problem is deemed to be oppression, and the solution is opposition (even of the violent type, if necessary) against the established oppressors. This might extend to authority structures the established oppressors have put into place to maintain the existing social order, including law enforcement (which is not to deny that law enforcement has been genuinely guilty of oppression at times). The traditional family might also be seen as an oppressive construct, as opposed to being something conceived by God.

According to this view, oppressed groups have more moral authority to speak to issues of justice. The Bible, which is the proper source of all moral authority and the standard for true justice, states that all lives are significant because all people are created in the image of God. When we lose the concept that all people are created in the image of God (at the point of conception), we lose the concept of their essential dignity—all people of all races.[84] **The Bible plainly condemns oppression, or racism, by any group as being sin, which is the true, ultimate and universal human problem—Christ being the only true solution.[85] We are commanded to love our neighbors as ourselves** in both the Old and New Testaments (Mark 12:31), and when asked, "Who then is my neighbor?" Jesus responded with the Parable of the Good Samaritan (Luke 10:25-37). It was the "unclean" Samaritan, rather than the self-righteous priest or the Levite, who fulfilled God's will in caring for the injured man

---

[84] An idea advanced by Francis Schaeffer in his book *Escape From Reason* (Downers Grove, IL: Intervarsity Press, 1968), p. 24.

[85] It is also worth noting that one in every eight Christians worldwide is currently being persecuted for their faith, with North Korea, Iran and Pakistan being the worst offenders (from Voice of the Martyrs). Little seems to be heard about this in the mainstream media.

beside the road. Samaritans as a racial group were despised by many Jews of the time.

Some of the sweetest fellowship I have known or witnessed has been between Christians of different races. At a time recently when social tensions were at a peak in this country, I witnessed our pastor stand in front of our congregation and call several members to join him at the front, among whom were an African-American member (who is also a deacon in our church) and a law enforcement officer (who is also a member). These were seated. Our pastor then rolled up his sleeves, got down on his knees and washed their feet, following the example set by Jesus in John 13:1-17. Many tears were shed in the process. What an incredible image of Christlikeness and reconciliation! *World Magazine*, a bi-weekly Christian news publication, identified as its "Daniel of the Year" John Perkins, a ninety-year-old African-American "who grew up in Mississippi, fled from it because of racism…and returned to help his former neighbors stand up to oppressors and glorify God."[86] As a young man in the 1940s, his family suffered abuse at the hands of law enforcement officials, which claimed the life of his brother. When he returned to Mississippi in the 1970s, he himself suffered brutal abuse. Despite having reason to, Perkins resolved not to hate; instead, he resolved to stand up to his oppressors in a non-violent manner and went on to found health clinics, theology classes, a housing cooperative and a Christian Community Development Association. "His Christian emphasis on nonviolence and loving enemies is a message America and the world desperately need…."[87]

---

[86] Olasky, Marvin, "After an Election, Reconciliation?" *World Magazine*, 11 November 2020, pp. 56-63.
[87] Ibid., p. 61.

The Old Testament prophets resound with this theme of justice. In the book of Amos, we find God speaking as follows:

"I hate, I reject your festivals,
Nor do I delight in your solemn assemblies.
Even though you offer up to Me burnt offerings and your grain offerings,
I will not accept *them*;
And I will not *even* look at the peace offerings of your fatlings.
Take away from Me the noise of your songs;
I will not even listen to the sound of your harps.
But let justice roll down like waters
And righteousness like an ever-flowing stream." (Amos 5:21-24)

And in Isaiah we find the following (again, God is speaking):

"Is this not the fast which I choose,
To loosen the bonds of wickedness,
To undo the bands of the yoke,
And to let the oppressed go free
And break every yoke?
Is it not to divide your bread with the hungry
And bring the homeless poor into the house;
When you see the naked, to cover him;
And not to hide yourself from your own flesh?" (Isaiah 58: 6-7)

Little credit seems to be given by "social justice" advocates for the tremendous strides towards true equality and justice that have been made over the last 250 years, and the fact that Christians (or Christian ideology) played key roles in many of these reforms. In fact, over just the last two decades, Christians have grown to be perceived as being the "bad guys" by much of Western culture. It is beyond the scope of this book to trace the reasons behind this development, but it should be noted here that we will face an uphill struggle in convincing a watching world otherwise. We must seek to be the best "bad guys" we can possibly be by genuinely loving our neighbors.[88] **The bottom line is this: This God with Whom we seek to dwell is passionate about justice, and He expects us to be as well.**

> For thus says the high and exalted One
> Who lives forever, whose name is Holy,
> **"I dwell *on* a high and holy place,**
> **And *also* with the contrite and lowly of spirit**
> In order to revive the spirit of the lowly
> And to revive the heart of the contrite." (Isaiah 57:15)

> **He has told you, O man, what is good;**
> **And what does the Lord require of you**
> **But to do justice, to love kindness,**
> **And to walk humbly with your God?** (Micah 6:8)

2.3 Trusting God

Next to believing that the Bible is the inspired, inerrant Word of God, the most important issue to be resolved by anyone seeking to dwell with God is knowing whether He can be trusted, and understanding what it actually means to trust Him. Jerry Bridges gives a definitive answer to these questions in his book entitled *Trusting God.* I am indebted to him for much of what follows on

---

[88] Stephen McAlpine has written an excellent book discussing this topic, entitled *Being the Bad Guys: How to Live for Jesus in a World That Says You Shouldn't* (United Kingdom: The Good Book Company, 2021).

this topic.[89] Bridges makes a strong case for the doctrine of the meticulous providence of God (without actually using those words to identify the doctrine), a doctrine I hold to myself. Meticulous providence is the idea that God controls every detail of our lives for His glory and our good, where "good" means being conformed to the image of Christ (Romans 8:28-29, note especially verse 29). This would include situations we encounter which display no obvious purpose for good (where "good" means our own personal benefit or the benefit of others), as with a natural disaster. Bridges develops this idea with an examination of the case of Job. Job never got an answer to the "why" questions he asked of God. God was meticulously controlling the details of his circumstances, and only the readers of this account in the Book of Job are privy to these details of God's actions.[90] As stated in the above section, the two essential truths about God for anyone seeking to dwell with Him are (1) that He is omniscient and omnipotent, and (2) that He is good and loving. An all-powerful and all-knowing God who is not meticulously loving and good in His dealings with man is a Deist God, not the God of the Bible. I would say that the majority of people who claim to be Christians in the world today are practical Deists.[91] On the other hand, a loving/good God who is ignorant of the details or powerless to

---

[89] Bridges was a staff member of the Navigators (a Christian organization focusing on one-on-one discipleship) and author who died in 1986, at the age of 86. His classic book *Trusting God* was published by NAVPRESS, Colorado Springs, in 1988.

[90] The identity of the book's author is uncertain. Even if the author were Job, there is no indication he knew the details of God's behind-the-scenes actions as they were unfolding.

[91] Once one has disavowed the God of the Bible, that person is then free to define God to suit personal preferences. It can readily be seen how this might then complement embracing self-actualization as a personal goal/idol (refer to Chapter 1.3, where idols are identified as a primary hindrance in dwelling with the one true God).

change them is an impotent God; again, not the God of the Bible.[92] The one who wants to dwell with God must seek to know the true God of the Bible. I have found it helpful to think of God being present in every detail, by distinguishing His **omnipresence** (as seen in Psalms 139) from His **manifest presence**, first at the burning bush, then at Sinai, then at the Red Sea and the mercy seat, and finally in the incarnation of Christ in Jesus ("The Word was God…and [He] became flesh and dwelt among us" [John 1:14]) and at Pentecost. He is manifestly present when it is obvious to us. But we must also know that while it will not always be obvious to us, **He is always there**, sovereignly superintending the details—that's meticulous providence. That brings up a point for which many will balk: **when bad things happen, we must assume that God is sovereign over them.** The following verses and quotes from Bridges' book attest to this:

> *If there is a single event in all the universe outside of God's sovereign control then we cannot trust Him.* (Bridges 37, emphasis in the original)

> We admit that we are often unable to reconcile God's sovereignty and goodness in the face of widespread tragedy or personal adversity, but we believe that, although we often do not understand God's ways, He is sovereignly at work in all of our circumstances. (Bridges 32)

> Therefore, those also who suffer according to the will of God shall entrust their souls to a faithful Creator in doing what is right. (I Peter 4:19)

---

[92] Such is the God of Rabbi Harold Kushner's bestselling book *When Bad Things Happen to Good People.*

....These things I have spoken to you, so that in Me you may have peace. In the world you have tribulation, but take courage; I have overcome the world. (John 16:33)

In the day of prosperity be happy,
But in the day of adversity consider—
God has made the one as well as the other
So that man will not discover anything *that will be* after him.
(Ecclesiastes 7:14)

The One forming light and creating darkness,
Causing well-being and creating calamity;
I am the Lord who does all these. (Isaiah 45:7)

Is it not from the mouth of the Most High
That both good and ill go forth? (Lamentations 3:38)

"For My thoughts are not your thoughts, / Nor are your ways My ways," declares the Lord. "For *as* the heavens are higher than the earth, / So are My ways higher than your ways / And My thoughts than your thoughts." (Isaiah 55:8-9)

Or do you suppose that those eighteen upon whom the Tower in Siloam fell and killed them were worse culprits than all the men in Judea? (Luke 13:1-5)

As I write this, the coronavirus pandemic has left in its wake over twenty-eight million people in this country who have been infected by the disease, and over half a million who have died from it. Those numbers only continue to climb. The pandemic has dramatically altered everyday life and business in every country in the world. In addition, this past week a tornado outbreak devastated the southern United States, leaving thirty-five people dead. In my state alone there were at least fifteen separate tornadoes on the ground in one evening. In fact, there were thirty named storms, including six hurricanes in the Atlantic basin, this year. The devastation in Central America was particularly heavy. The question many are asking is, "Where is God in all of this?" I don't have any grand, ultimate explanation of why God has allowed these things to happen; although, I do actually see some good that is coming out of it all.[93] For example, Samaritan's Purse flew their DC-8 cargo jet to Honduras to airlift their emergency field hospital, complete with doctors and nurses, water-filtration systems and a helicopter for access to remote locations, and they have on more than one occasion rushed to set up field hospitals for COVID relief in other areas.

All I can do is hold onto the truths from Scripture that God has given us about Himself. As I write this this morning, I received Paul David Tripp's weekly devotional email, "Wednesday's Word."[94] He quotes Matthew 10:29, in which Jesus says, "Are not two sparrows sold for a penny? And not one of them will fall to the ground apart from your father" (ESV). Tripp cites the statistic that 13.7 million birds die in the United States every day. Why isn't that reported on the evening news? Because few people care. And yet God is in active control over every aspect of those birds' lives, up to and including their deaths. That's meticulous grace, meticulous providence. Jesus goes on to say, "But even the hairs of your head are numbered. Fear not, therefore; you are of more

---

[93] John Piper, in his helpful book *The Coronavirus and Christ* (Wheaton, IL: Crossway, 2020), identifies six possible positive outcomes of the pandemic (reasoning, as he does, from Scripture); and Erwin Lutzer in his book, *Pandemics, Plagues and Natural Disasters: What Is God Saying to Us?* (Chicago: Moody Publishers, 2020), identifies five things God is saying to us through the virus, also based completely upon Scripture.

[94] Paul Tripp, "Wednesday's Word," <paultripp.com/wednesdays-word>. April 15, 2020.

value than many sparrows" (Matthew 10:30-31, ESV). Creation has been groaning since The Fall, and we ourselves groan (Romans 8:19-23). Yet the whole time God has remained in control, bringing all things to an ultimate "summing-up of all things in Christ" (Ephesians 1:10), and the whole time devoting His special attention to those who seek to dwell in Him. So, should I pray about the coronavirus? Absolutely. About a parking place? By all means, but all the time doing what I can to obtain the best result (as in "social distancing" and wearing a mask for the pandemic) and being ready to accept whatever He delivers, knowing that He has my long-term best interests at heart.

These are probably the most difficult truths in all of Scripture, but they are there for us to reckon with. If that sounds difficult to do, we must realize that it is only possible to trust God one step at a time, just as we obey Him one step at a time. We must never glibly try to pass these truths along to others, particularly to those who may be suffering or grieving, however necessary they (these truths) may be for one seeking to know and dwell with the one true God of the Bible.

> Let no unwholesome word proceed from your mouth, but only such a word as is good for edification according to the need *of the moment*, so that it will give grace to those who hear. (Ephesians 4:29)

I am reminded of the account in John 11 of Jesus deliberately delaying his arrival at the call for Him to come and heal His friend Lazarus, who then, in Jesus' prolonged absence, died and was buried. When Jesus did finally arrive, He raised Lazarus from the dead, but not before weeping over his death. I am able to see that, while Jesus was completely in control of the entire ordeal, He allowed Lazarus to suffer to serve a larger purpose (in which

Lazarus benefitted—he was healed), and He did deeply grieve over Lazarus' suffering. He did not glibly dismiss the suffering as being necessary. At the same time, He used the event as a demonstration of His omnipotence. "**I am** the resurrection and the life." He is our great hope, even in the face of death. We are often able to see God's purposes in retrospect, but even when we cannot, we can know they are always ultimately for His glory and our good, and that He deeply cares for us in all situations of adversity and distress. Joseph is another great example of this. Sold into slavery by his brothers, he ultimately rose to a high position within the Egyptian kingdom, through God's meticulous providence (although not without "setbacks" along the way). When a famine struck the entire area (again, through God's meticulous providence), his brothers appeared before him seeking food, which he had in abundance, yet again through God's meticulous providence. He said to his brothers, "As for you, you meant evil against me, but God meant it **for good**, to bring it about that many people should be kept alive, as they are today" (Genesis 50:20). God superintended the whole story "**for good**."

So, what does trusting God look like, on a moment-by-moment basis, for us in New Testament times? As was stated at the beginning of this section, trusting Him is essential for anyone wishing to dwell with Him. When an issue arises that requires our trust, I believe we must first make a decision to trust Him, and then go on record as having done so. This I do by writing it out in my journal, but it may also be done by prayer (preferably out loud). I am reminded of Joshua's declaration, "…as for me and my house, we will serve the Lord!" (Joshua 24:15) and Martin Luther's famous statement, "Here I stand!" before his trial for heresy—each a bold declaration in the face of a situation that would impress weaker souls to **not** trust God. Next, **the principle of living in "day-tight increments" should be applied**. This is the concept in

Matthew 6:34: "So do not worry about tomorrow; for tomorrow will care for itself. Each day has enough trouble of its own." This I try to accomplish by writing out a simple agenda for each day, a list I label "Day's Own Trouble" or simply "DOT" in my journal or to-do list. I then commit the list to the LORD and check them off as they are done. In the process, I have trusted God in both the things I could do and the things that are for the time being beyond me. For those of you who may have already had the opportunity to read **Appendix 2** by this point, it is worth noting that this differs from simply being myopic by the very fact that we do know Who holds our future, and **He is completely dependable and trustworthy**. Big difference. That is to say, we **do** plan for the future where we may, by the wisdom He gives us, but then we leave those plans in His hands. James 4:13-15 gives us the following admonition:

> Come now, you who say, "Today or tomorrow we will go to such and such a city, and spend a year there and engage in business and make a profit." Yet you do not know what your life will be like tomorrow. You are *just* a vapor that appears for a little while and then vanishes away. Instead, *you ought* to say, "If the Lord wills, we will live and also do this or that."

Now the question arises about how to process setbacks. Setbacks I simply add to the end of my master list—perhaps including one or two of them on the next day's DOT list. Before I go to bed each evening I "roll" the burden of the unfinished list off onto the LORD's broad shoulders: "Therefore humble yourselves under the mighty hand of God, that He may exalt you at the proper time, **casting [literally rolling off] all your anxiety on Him**, because He cares for you" (I Peter 5:6-7). What is that, I ask you, if not trusting God (and **dwelling** in Him in the process)? This makes me further appreciate God's wisdom in His design of the universe to have our lives ordered in a daily cycle of wakefulness and sleep, a regular rhythm of engagement and withdrawal.[95] I just need to ensure that my withdrawal is always into the ready arms of Christ and not into myself or the desires of my flesh (sin nature).

One final thought on trusting God before we move on. We must always bear in mind Who Jesus is—He is both our intercessor (Hebrews 7:25) and our advocate (I John 2:1). As our intercessor before God's throne, He "always lives to make intercession for [us]." He can do this because His blood is the propitiation for our sins. Dane Ortlund writes:

> Intercession has the idea of mediating between two parties, bringing them together. Advocacy is similar but has the idea of aligning oneself with another. An intercessor stands between two parties; an advocate doesn't simply stand in between two parties but steps over and joins the one party as he approaches the other. Jesus is not only an intercessor but an advocate…. Jesus shares with us in our actual experience. He feels what we feel. He draws near. And He speaks up longingly on our behalf.[96]

We can trust God because we have an understanding advocate standing in His presence with us Who is, Himself, God. Please let that incredible, mind-boggling truth sink in for a moment. What more could we ask? That's a God we can trust!

---

[95] Nuenke, Doug and Pam. "Rhythms of Engagement and Withdrawal," Originally from *Christian Living*, 1 January 2015. Published online by the Navigators, accessed on 8 January 2021 <navigators.org/rhythms-of-engagement-and-withdrawal>.
[96] Ortlund, Dane. *Gentle and Lowly: The Heart of Christ for Sinners and Sufferers* (Wheaton, IL: Crossway, 2020), pp. 87, 89.

2.4 God's Plan All Along

So, God created man to enjoy the glory of His presence, but that project was disrupted when man rebelled against God. **All sin is, ultimately, rebellion against the revealed, known will of God.** "God wants (A), BUT I want (B). And I choose (B) because He has disappointed me once too often in the past, or because basically I no longer fear Him that much. And besides, if I should ever have to face His judgement in the future, He will have to concede I'm not as bad as most others are, or because (B) is not as bad as (C)." At least, that became my preferred line of thinking, and the Bible says it is "common to man [that means women, too]" (I Corinthians 10:13). That obviously disrupts our intimacy (**dwelling**) with God, who is holy and perfect. That's the story in Genesis 3, when Adam and Eve were expelled from the Garden, and has been the story ever since. And He has ever since been providing a way for us to reconnect and, once again, **dwell** with Him. It has always required both repentance and faith on our part, but the content of that required faith (the articles of that faith) has changed, up until the canon of Scripture was closed around 100 AD with John's Revelation. For example, Abraham "saw Christ's day" (John 8:56) from a distance, but could not have given the many specifics of His identity, crucifixion or resurrection. Later, the prophets often had only a limited understanding of the details of their own prophecies. What a blessing to have the details we now have! Peter tells us,

> As to this salvation, the prophets who prophesied of the grace that would come to you made careful searches and inquiries, seeking to know what person or time the Spirit of Christ within them was indicated as He predicted the sufferings of Christ and the glories to follow. It was revealed to them that they were not serving themselves, but you, in these things which now have been announced to you through those who have preached the

gospel to you by the Holy Spirit sent from heaven—things into which angels long to look (I Peter 1:10-12).

Rahab the harlot is cited in the "Faith Hall of Fame" in Hebrews 11, but she knew none of the specific details about the Messiah. Hebrews 11:39-40 tells us regarding all of the heroes of the faith listed in Hebrews 11, "And all these, having gained approval through their faith, did not receive what was promised, because God had provided something better for us, so that apart from us they would not be made perfect." Any individual Old Testament Hebrew presenting an offering in the temple knew few, if any, of the specific details of Jesus of Nazareth's life and ministry.[97] Now those details "have once for all been delivered to the Saints" (Jude 3). Their faith looked forward, and ours looks backward to the cross; in both cases, the faith is honored by God and "reckoned as righteousness" (Romans 4:3). Throughout the Old Testament, we see God progressively revealing more truth about Himself, and then holding His people accountable for the truth he had revealed. Early on He revealed His sovereignty (over the Egyptian army) and His authority (through Moses and the law), making clear that there could be no remission of sin without the shedding of blood (His holiness). That's what the sacrifices were all about. But don't miss the fact that He **dwelt** among them in the pillar of smoke and fire, and made a way for them to approach Him in the tabernacle and later the temple. The design of these structures illustrates the requirements for Him to be able to **dwell** among His people—His holiness and His provision for His sinful people to approach Him

---

[97] As early as the Garden of Eden, God's statement to the Serpent revealed that "the seed of the woman would crush the Serpent's head." This is referred to as the *Protoevangelium*. And, of course, the prophets predicted the suffering of the Messiah (as in Isaiah 53) and His reign as king in the End Times, but the point made here is that none had the specific details of His identity as Jesus of Nazareth.

in repentance and faith in His mercy and grace. He manifested His "shekinah" glory at the point where the wings of the two cherubim facing each other touch each other on the lid of the Ark of the Covenant (the mercy seat) in the Holy of Holies. The word *shekinah* is not found in the Bible, only in the Talmud (a collection of Jewish civil and ceremonial law and legend comprising the Mishnah and the Gemara, written in Aramaic after the close of the Christian Biblical canon); but it is interesting nonetheless, because its basic meaning is the dwelling or settling of the divine presence.

God chose Jerusalem as His eternal **dwelling** place (Psalms 132:13-14). I believe the Bible teaches that Jesus will yet return to the Mount of Olives (Zechariah 13:4), enter Jerusalem through its reopened Eastern Gate, and then **dwell** and reign for a thousand years (the "Millennium") from that city (Revelation 20).[98] Even afterward in eternity, after all the elements "pass away with intense heat" (II Peter) and the earth is recreated, the New Jerusalem will descend upon it (Revelation 22). I say, "Come quickly, Lord Jesus," (Revelation 22:20) but graciously He dwells (here meaning tarries) so that all his elect may enter His kingdom.[99] "In my Father's house are many dwelling places..." said Jesus (John 14:2). Our pastor has a timeline that he rehearses with the children frequently, during the time each Sunday he calls them to the front. This timeline traces events in the Bible from creation to eternity (and he does this in less than two minutes!), presenting strong

---

[98] This is according to the Pre-Millennial view of the End Times. Refer to **Appendix 4** for an explanation/overview of the End Times from a pre-millennial perspective. **Appendix 3** is a graphic depiction of how God's covenant promises will be fulfilled.

[99] If you are worried the least bit about whether you may or may not be one of God's elect, then that's a good indication God may be calling you—so why not respond now in repentance and faith and settle the whole question for all eternity? (John 3:16)

evidence to our entire congregation that **God's plan all along has been to dwell with His people and to be their true home**.

In fact, God has stated over forty times in both the Old and New Testaments that His intention is to have a people for His own possession among whom He may **dwell**. Quoting from Exodus, where God expressed His desire to dwell among His people in the tabernacle He instructed them to build, Paul writes to the Corinthians:

> Or what agreement has the temple of God with idols? For we are the temple of the living God; just as God said, "I will **dwell** in them and walk among them; / And I will be their God, and they shall be My people." (II Corinthians 6:16)

The point Paul makes is that we are now, ourselves, that tabernacle! But in the End Times, as John states, He will once again physically dwell among us:

> And I heard a loud voice from the throne, saying, "Behold, the tabernacle of God is among men, and He will **dwell** among them, and they shall be His people, and God Himself will be among them…" (Revelation 21:3)

That will be a glorious time for us (the Church) as we co-reign with Christ, but also for the House of Israel when God completes the covenant He had made with them.

> "For this is the covenant that I will make with the house of Israel
> After those days, says the Lord:
>
> I will put My laws into their minds,
> And I will write them on their hearts.

And I will be their God,
And they shall be My people. (Hebrews 8:10)

And, again, in Ezekiel 37:26-27:

> I will make a covenant of peace with them; it will be an everlasting covenant with them. And I will place them and multiply them, and will set My sanctuary in their midst forever. My **dwelling** place also will be with them; and I will be their God, and they will be My people.

Applying that same concept to the New Testament Church, in which He currently dwells:

> But you are a chosen race, a royal priesthood, a holy nation, a people for *God's* own possession, so that you may proclaim the excellencies of Him who has called you out of darkness into His marvelous light; for you once were not a people, but now you are the people of God; you had not received mercy, but now you have received mercy. (I Peter 2:9-10)

We, the Church,[100] are a people for God's own possession right now! And someday soon He will be present with us again physically: "I will **dwell** among them, and I will be their God, and they will be my people" (II Corinthians 6:16 and Revelation 21:3)—that's what I'm waiting for! Come quickly, Lord Jesus!

What follows in Part II is a discussion of twelve other commands found in Scripture (**abide**, **wait**, watch, **pray**, fast, **worship**, **rest**, **study**, **meditate**, sit, **walk** and stand). The eight listed in bold font are considered to be core, while the remaining four are necessary

---

[100] **Appendix 5** is a consideration of how God is actively dwelling in His Church today.

to discuss in order to clearly understand those that are core. These eight other commands were selected for their congruence with the concept of dwelling in Christ. It must be acknowledged that the list used is not exhaustive. There are, for instance, commands to rejoice ("Rejoice in the Lord always, again I say rejoice..." [Philippians 4:4]) and to go ("Go therefore and make disciples of all nations..." [Matthew 28:19]). I would suggest, however, that if one were to focus on keeping these core eight commands, that person would find himself or herself rejoicing and going as well.

2.5 For Further Thought

1. Why should we need to find refuge in God?

2. What is "meticulous providence," and what does it mean to trust God? How would it affect our daily lives if we embraced this doctrine?

3. How might the strategy of "living in day-tight increments" assist you in trusting God?

4. What is a theodicy, and what might yours be?

5. How might it be said that God's plan all along has been to dwell with His people and to be their true home?

Part II

Other Scriptural Mandates Related to Dwelling: Abide, Wait, Pray, Worship, Rest, Study, Meditate, Walk

Chapter 3

Abide

If you abide in Me, and My words abide in you, ask whatever you wish, and it will be done for you. (John 15:7)

This brings us to the second command for one seeking to dwell in Christ, to abide. How is the concept of abiding in Christ (and having Him abide in us) related to the concept of dwelling? It would appear that Psalms 91:1 gives us an answer:

He who dwells in the shelter of the Most High
Will abide in the shadow of the Almighty.

In other words, as indicated by the words in bold font above, dwelling and abiding are largely synonymous. Let's examine these two words more carefully.

I believe in a doctrine called "The Security of the Believer," or to use a phrase more often heard, "Once Saved, Always Saved." John 10:27-29 says the following:

My sheep hear My voice, and I know them, and they follow Me; and I give eternal life to them, and they will never perish; and no one will snatch them out of My hand. My Father, who has given *them* to Me, is greater than all; and no one is able to snatch *them* out of the Father's hand.

This verse tells us that we are securely in God's hands if we have repented and believe in Christ and committed our lives to him as Lord. No person or power is able to snatch us away from that security, and "in His presence is fullness of joy" (Psalms 16:11).

Also, in Ephesians 1:13-14 we find:

In Him, you also, after listening to the message of truth, the gospel of your salvation—having also believed, you were sealed in Him with the Holy Spirit of promise, who is given as a pledge of our inheritance, with a view to the redemption of *God's own* possession, to the praise of His glory.

The pledge referred to in this verse is actually the image of earnest money (in this case of course it is the Spirit Himself and not money) given as a down-payment for our full inheritance, which we shall receive at His coming (or at our death, whichever occurs first) at which point we shall begin dwelling with Him face-to-face. The seal is the official guarantee of the genuineness of our inheritance, as a seal in New Testament times was placed on an official document certifying its authenticity.

In Romans 8:31-39 we find this:

What then shall we say to these things? If God *is* for us, who *is* against us? He who did not spare His own Son, but delivered Him over for us all, how will He not also with Him freely give us all things? Who will bring a charge against God's elect?

God is the one who justifies; who is the one who condemns? Christ Jesus is He who died, yes, rather who was raised, who is at the right hand of God, who also intercedes for us. Who will separate us from the love of Christ? Will tribulation, or distress, or persecution, or famine, or nakedness, or peril, or sword?

The answer to each of these rhetorical questions is "no person or thing is able to separate us from the love of Christ."

And finally, in Ephesians 2:4-7 we find:

But God, being rich in mercy, because of His great love with which He loved us, even when we were dead in our transgressions, made us alive together with Christ (by grace you have been saved), and raised us up with Him, and seated us with Him in the heavenly *places* in Christ Jesus, so that in the ages to come He might show the surpassing riches of His grace in kindness toward us in Christ Jesus.

So, the believer has been **seated** in the heavenly places and **sealed** with the Holy Spirit of promise. No person or power may snatch us out of Christ's hand. That is our **position**. It is where we dwell. Psalms 23:6 tells us that we will dwell in the house of the Lord forever. Our **walk**, on the other hand, may at times be less than perfectly according to God's will as we move through the sanctification process. More will be said about our walk in **Chapter 7**, and **Appendix 9** is a graphical explanation of what happens when and after we are saved (justified through the imputed righteousness of Christ). Once this has occurred, we may at times fall out of close fellowship with God and not be abiding in Him, but our position will never change. This is analogous to our U.S. citizenship, which remains in full force and effect when we leave this country. Philippians 3:20 says "our citizenship is in heaven." As the terms are used Biblically, *dwelling* seems to be used more to refer to our position, and *abiding* more to our walk. **Appendix 1** gives more detail on how these words are used and their meanings in the original languages in the Bible, but here we may note the following:

- **Dwelling** is more about where I am in eternity (my position).

- **Abiding** is more about where I am at any given time (my walk).

Seen in this light, dwelling is a broader concept than abiding. In other words, dwelling is everything that abiding is plus more. It would not be possible to abide without also dwelling. That is, if any believer has ever truly abided in Christ through accepting Christ as Lord and Savior, that person will continue to dwell. However, if a born-again believer were out of fellowship with God, God would still be dwelling in that person and that person would still be seated in the heavenlies with Christ, but that person would not be abiding in Christ. As the words are used Biblically, *dwelling* refers to a more permanent, settled arrangement. All true believers are dwelling, but not all are abiding at any given time; on the other hand, all who are abiding are also dwelling.

This could be illustrated graphically as follows, where the circles represent the domain of meaning of each word as it is used in the Bible:

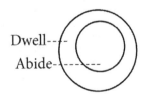

This is not, however, the case with the remaining seven activities we will look at: wait, pray, worship, rest, study, meditate and walk. These are all somewhat synonymous with dwelling, but their individual domains of meaning do not form concentric circles with dwell, as does abide; they merely overlap—some to greater degrees than others. That is, they can each also mean things distinct in meaning from dwelling. They are congruous enough, however, to be considered actions of someone who is dwelling in Christ.

As the terms are used Biblically, to dwell, as we have seen, is to settle in and make ourselves at home, to live, to reside and enjoy the protection of the place. Abide means to wait or endure in expectation, or without yielding. Dwelling denotes more of a long-term commitment, whereas abiding is more of a moment-by-moment endeavor. **This is not to suggest, however, that dwelling is merely a once-and-done matter. For believers, it is a reality we should continue to celebrate, own, enjoy, take comfort in and be thankful for, to "take full possession of" and live to the full advantage of or to find rest in.** We are to seek to "dwell in His tent and take refuge in the shadow of His wings" (Psalms 61:4). These are the active steps a believer takes as outlined in **Chapter 2**—our part in dwelling in Him. We are to step under the protection of the "shelter of our Most High God" (Psalms 91:1) and remain there at all times. We are to continually examine and ask ourselves, "Am I doing that? Am I actively dwelling?" Dwelling implies a dwelling place (either figurative, as with a New Testament believer in Christ being the dwelling place of God's Spirit; or literal, as with the Israelites dwelling in the Old Testament's Promised Land), while abiding suggests a vital connection (as with a branch to a vine). The phrase "dwelling place" occurs frequently in the Bible, but never do we find "abiding place." Witness Lee (a Taiwanese Christian preacher who died in 1997) said, **"If you abide in a certain place for a few days and then leave, that is not a home to you, but a hotel or a motel. Unfortunately, many Christians abide in Christ as a motel, just for a temporary stay. But we need to get ourselves settled in Christ, to make Christ our home. We need to dwell in Him.... Our real and permanent home is our God. Christ is our home and our dwelling place."**[101] The LORD promised Moses and Joshua that he was giving them the Promised Land as a place in which they could dwell and find rest. We may enter that same rest today by believing and dwelling in Christ (Hebrews 4).[102] As with the Promised Land of the Israelites, we flourish in our New Testament promised land when we recognize the boundaries and prohibitions God has instituted. We carry our promised land with us everywhere we go. Ours transcends geography—that's real dwelling!

As was the case with dwelling, abiding is a reciprocal activity. The abode that we have in Christ and that He has in us is a mutual abode. John 14:23 says,

> Jesus answered and said to him, "If anyone loves Me, he will keep My word; and My Father will love him, and We will come to him and make Our **abode** with him."

Probably the defining passage on our abiding in Christ comes from John 15:1-11:[103]

---

[101] Lee, Witness. "Abiding, Dwelling, and Making Home in Christ," excerpt from *The Secret of Experiencing Christ*. Living Stream Ministry, 28 April 2020. <ministrysamples.org>

[102] More on the concept of resting follows in **Chapter 5**.

[103] Jesus tells us in this passage to "abide **in Me**." The phrase *in Christ* is used 164 times in the Apostle Paul's letters, the Book of Ephesians primary among them, where it is used 75 times. This underscores the importance of the concept

I am the true vine, and My Father is the vinedresser. Every branch in Me that does not bear fruit, He takes away; and every *branch* that bears fruit, He prunes it so that it may bear more fruit. You are already clean because of the word which I have spoken to you. **Abide** in Me, and I in you. As the branch cannot bear fruit of itself unless it **abides** in the vine, so neither *can* you unless you **abide** in Me. I am the vine, you are the branches; he who **abides** in Me and I in him, he bears much fruit, for apart from Me you can do nothing. If anyone does not **abide** in Me, he is thrown away as a branch and dries up; and they gather them, and cast them into the fire and they are burned. If you **abide** in Me, and My words **abide** in you, ask whatever you wish, and it will be done for you. My Father is glorified by this, that you bear much fruit, and *so* prove to be My disciples. Just as the Father has loved Me, I have also loved you; **abide** in My love. If you keep My commandments, you will **abide** in My love; just as I have kept My Father's commandments and **abide** in His love. These things I have spoken to you so that My joy may be in you, and *that* your joy may be made full.

What is immediately obvious from the above passage is how central the Word of God is to the process of abiding (see also John 14:21, 23). "His words" must abide in us, but (and this is key) what should continually draw us back into the Scriptures should be a Holy Spirit-inspired hunger and thirst and not a legalistic, compulsive burden to check off another box on a to-do list. We

---

of being **in Christ** to dwelling and abiding. As stated earlier in **Chapter 2.1, our goal is not merely to move closer to Christ, but to dwell in Him, to abide in Him.** While it is true that James 4:8 says, "Draw near to God, and He will draw near to you," the rest of that same verse makes it clear that the drawing near referred to here is a complete surrender to dwell in Christ (not just near him). "Cleanse your hands you sinners, and **purify your hearts you double-minded.**"

will then know we are abiding in Him when He produces fruit through us and in us. This fruit will be more evident in what we are becoming than in what we are doing. This is not to say that discipline is not involved in studying and meditating on Scripture, just that we are being led by the Spirit and get a joy from doing it. More will be said in **Chapter 6** about how we can effectively study and meditate on scripture.

In addition to the forty occurrences of the word *abide* in the Gospel of John, the Johannine letters contain twenty-nine occurrences, chief among them being the following. John, who was most likely in his eighties at the time, was writing against the spread of Greek Gnosticism in the church.[104]

> What was from the beginning, what we have heard, what we have seen with our eyes, what we have looked at and touched with our hands, concerning the Word of Life— and the life was manifested, and we have seen and testify and proclaim to you the eternal life, which was with the Father and was manifested to us— what we have seen and heard we proclaim to you also, so that you too may have fellowship with us; and indeed our fellowship is with the Father, and with His Son Jesus Christ. (I John 1:1-3)

> As for you, let that abide in you which you heard from the beginning. If what you heard from the beginning abides in you, you also will abide in the Son and in the Father. (I John 2:24)

---

[104] In a simple summary, the Greek Gnostics believed that "humans are divine souls trapped in an ordinary physical (material) world." (From Wikipedia <en.wikipedia.org/wiki/Gnosticism>, accessed 25 July 2021.) Humans are able to transcend this trap by attaining secret, mystical knowledge of a divine being, who was not the God of the Bible.

The one who keeps His commandments abides in Him, and He in him. We know by this that He abides in us, by the Spirit whom He has given us. (I John 3:24)

So, John teaches us that Jesus was the one true God in real (tangible) human flesh (and that was good, not bad), abiding is a reciprocal relationship (as with dwelling), the abiding presence of the Holy Spirit within us is our assurance of salvation, and spiritual knowledge or truth may be propositional, instead of merely mystical.

In summary, Chip Ingram puts it as follows:

God wants to produce in us what we don't have in ourselves. And the way it happens is through *abiding*. To abide or "remain" means we're *connected* to God. It doesn't mean everything is always going great, and it doesn't mean we have ooey-gooey feelings toward Him all the time. But it does mean that we're on the same page. We know that we're abiding when we're led to pray in ways that we didn't pray before. And as we get nearer to God's heart, we find that our will begins to align more with His will. Our focus isn't on doing more, but *being* more. We can truly abide with God when our heart, our life, and our relationship with Jesus is our first priority.[105]

Notice the emphasis Ingram puts upon heart and relationship as key factors in abiding. More will be said about this in **Chapter 5**, on resting in our relationship with Christ.

---

[105] Ingram, Chip. "God's Number One Goal for Your Life." Living on the Edge, 20 July 2020. <livingontheedge.org/2019/05/01/gods-number-one-goal-for-your-life/>

For Further Thought

1. What does it mean to abide in Christ?

2. How can I know that I am abiding in Christ (refer to the quote from Chip Ingram above)?

3. What distinguishes abiding from dwelling? Please remember, **Appendix 1** is a word study on the words *abide* and *dwell*.

4. What is the central, essential element for abiding in Him (according to John 15:7, 10)?

5. What is significant about the preposition *in*, as it relates to the concept of abiding **in** Christ? How is being **in** Him distinguished from merely seeking to "draw closer to Him"? Which is the Biblical ideal? How is the distinction here related to our earlier discussion of the word *integrity*? Hint: How is the phrase *all-in* connected to the concept of abiding in Christ? Why does abiding in Christ require integrity? (Refer to **Chapter 1.2.**)

Chapter 4

Wait, Watch, Pray, Fast and Worship

Yet those who wait for the Lord
Will gain new strength;
They will mount up with wings like eagles,
They will run and not get tired,
They will walk and not become weary. (Isaiah 40:31)

...pray without ceasing... (I Thessalonians 5:17)

_____

Waiting, as used in the Bible, is the confident expectation and anticipation of God's action to fulfill His promises. Waiting implies hope. Andree Sue Peterson, writing in *World* magazine, says, "Anticipation is in our nature, and our Creator wants it that way…. We are hardwired for goals, and the absence of them mitigates *shalom*…. It is the Master who has made us all this way. He has no interest in changing this peculiarity about us. He only wishes that anticipation would be fixed on things above, not on things below that pass away."[106] She cites the examples of Anna and Simeon waiting in the temple for the Messiah to appear. They literally **dwelt** in the temple in anticipation. What she says seems to also be confirmed by other passages, such as the following:

> I would have despaired unless I had believed that I would see the goodness of the LORD
> In the land of the living.
> **Wait** for the LORD;
> Be strong and let your heart take courage;
> Yes, **wait** for the LORD. (Psalms 27:13-14)

> I **wait** for the LORD, my soul does **wait**,
> And in His word do I hope.
> My soul **waits** for the Lord,
> More than the watchman for the morning
> O **Israel [Bob]** hope in the LORD;
> For with the Lord there is lovingkindness.
> And with Him is abundant redemption.
> And he will redeem **Israel [Bob]**. (Psalms 130:5-6)

Based upon Ephesians 1:4 (that I am also, now, God's "chosen"), I have taken the liberty of writing in my own name above the word *Israel* in the above passage in my Bible, for I have been grafted in to the promises God gave to Israel, as explained in Romans 9-11[107]

---

[106] Peterson, Andree Sue, "Looking Forward," *World*, 7 December 2019, p. 63.

[107] I am not saying here that the Church has replaced Israel in God's scheme of events for the End Times. It has not. We (the Church) are just now included in these particular promises God made to Israel (see Ephesians 2). That is the mystery Paul refers to. The ancient prophets saw the Church vaguely, much as a valley between the mountaintops of the first and second comings, and easily conflated the two comings into the same event (see **Appendix 3** for a graphic explanation). An example of this is found in Isaiah 61. Jesus read from this Scripture from the scroll in Nazareth (in Luke 4), but stopped in the middle of a

and Ephesians 2-3. The word "lovingkindness" (*hesed*) above is the Hebrew word for God's covenantal love which He bestows upon Israel (and upon anyone who is in Christ). Lamentations 3:21-25 says,

> Surely my soul remembers
> And is bowed down within me.
> This I recall to mind;
> Therefore, I have hope.
>
> The Lord's lovingkindnesses indeed never cease,
> For His compassions never fail.
> *They* are new every morning;
> Great is Your faithfulness.
>
> "The Lord is my portion," says my soul,
> "Therefore I have hope in Him."
> The Lord is good to those who **wait** for Him,
> To the person who seeks Him.
>
> *It is* good that he **waits** silently
> For the salvation of the Lord. (Lamentations 3:21-26)

In this particular case His promise comes to the prophet's mind as the nation is being sent into exile, after having seen Jerusalem and their temple destroyed. What better case could we find of someone waiting, taking his soul in-hand, based upon God's promises and His character? This idea of waiting on the LORD is woven all through the psalms and the prophets, as evidenced below:

<del>sentence describing both the first and second comings (Verses 1 and 2). See</del> **Appendix 4** for a graphic explanation.

Yet those who **wait** for the Lord
Will gain new strength;
They will mount up *with* wings like eagles,
They will run and not get tired,
They will walk and not become weary. (Isaiah 40:31)

Make me know Your ways, O LORD;
Teach me Your paths.
Lead me in Your truth and teach me,
For You are the God of my salvation:
For You I **wait** all the day. (Psalms 25:4-5)

I **wait** for the Lord, my soul does **wait**,
And in His word do I hope.
My soul **waits** for the Lord
More than the watchmen for the morning;
Indeed, more than the watchmen for the morning.
O Israel, hope in the Lord;
For with the Lord there is lovingkindness,
And with Him is abundant redemption. (Psalms 130:5-7)

He does not delight in the strength of the horse;
He does not take pleasure in the legs of a man.

The Lord favors those who fear Him,
Those who **wait** for His lovingkindness.

Praise the Lord, O Jerusalem!
Praise your God, O Zion! (Psalms 147:10-12)

My soul *waits* in silence for God only;
From Him is my salvation.
He only is my rock and my salvation,
My stronghold; I shall not be greatly shaken. (Psalms 62:1-2)

I find a strong connection in the Scriptures between waiting on the LORD and pouring out one's soul before Him. Psalms 62 (quoted above) goes on to say in verse 8, "Trust in Him at all times, O people; / Pour out your heart before Him; / God is a refuge for us." That verse makes me thankful that He cares, understands and will listen to us, but we have to make the time to go before Him in prayer and wait for Him to answer. In **Chapter 1.3**, we saw how **busyness** can be a **hindrance** for those desiring to **dwell** in God. The busy, fast-paced lifestyles of many people in this world today can make **waiting** (and spending time in prayer) seem difficult and odious. It is, nonetheless, imperative that we understand the importance from God's perspective of waiting, for it is in waiting that we learn to truly experience His faithfulness. Waiting is a crucial part of following after Him. Bradley Baurain, in his helpful book *On Waiting Well*, draws an interesting distinction between waiting **for** the LORD ("staying in a place literally or figuratively until a person arrives or an event occurs") as in Isaiah 40:31 above, and waiting **on** the LORD ("in the sense of attending to or serving" Him) as in the remaining passages above.[108] He further distinguishes between the waiting categories of "small w" (consisting of specific times or seasons) and "big W" (consisting of "worship-filled experiences of waiting on the Lord and delighting in His presence as a way of life").[109] Obviously, all of the above types of waiting are called for in a mature walk of faith. In answer to his own question, "What are we waiting for?" Baurain finds seven answers from Scripture: rescue, promises, salvation (including regeneration, sanctification and glorification—see **Appendix 9, Part II** for more details), justice, grace, forgiveness

---

[108] Baurain, Bradley. *On Waiting Well: Moving from Endurance to Enjoyment When You're Waiting on God* (Chicago: Moody Publishers, 2020), pp. 15, 21.
[109] ~~"In a Venn diagram, 'small w' waiting would be a small circle entirely~~ contained within a larger circle, 'big W' waiting." Ibid.

and Christ's return.[110] He concludes that the "what" (as in, "What are we waiting for?") becomes a "Whom" (Christ Himself) in answer to his own question. A great example of this type of waiting is seen in Joseph of Arimathea, who was "himself **waiting** for the kingdom of God" (Mark 15:43). He put himself at risk in asking for the body of Jesus following the crucifixion. He recognized that Jesus **was** the kingdom of God, the fulfillment of what he had been waiting for—the "what" was indeed a "Whom!"

Paul David Tripp writes that waiting for the kingdom of God "is not at all like the meaningless waiting you do at the doctor's office." Instead, waiting is our calling and blessing "because every one of God's children lives between the 'already' and the 'not yet'" aspects of God's kingdom:

> Already this world has been broken by sin, but not yet has it been made new again. Already has Jesus come, but not yet has He returned to take you home with Him forever. Already has your sin been forgiven, but not yet have you been fully delivered from it. Already Jesus reigns, but not yet has His final kingdom come. Already sin has been defeated, but not yet has it been completely destroyed. Already the Holy Spirit has been given, but not yet have you been perfectly formed into the likeness of Jesus. Already God has given you His word, but not yet has it totally transformed your life. Already you have been given grace, but not yet has that grace finished its work. You see, **we're all called to wait** because we all live right smack dab

---

[110] Ibid., pp. 86-112.

in the middle of God's grand redemptive story [emphasis added].[111]

As that story unfolds in Scripture, the one who waits is also often pictured as being either in distress or in eager expectation of rescue from an otherwise desperate situation. In such instances, the waiting is seen as being done in view of God's promise of rescue or deliverance. Another word often employed to express the same general idea is **watch**. Closely associated with this concept of waiting while in desperation is the image of being thirsty in a "dry and weary land," as in Psalms 63:1, 8—and here an example of all four types of waiting referred to above (a needy, desperate situation is at hand, and again the desired answer is the presence of the LORD, Himself):

> O God, You are my God; I shall seek You earnestly;
> My soul thirsts for You, my flesh yearns for You,
> In a dry and weary land where there is no water....
> My soul clings to You;
> Your right hand upholds me.

This is, again, the image of a soul in exile, in a land apart from God which can never satisfy one's deepest longings. Writing before the Southern Kingdom was carried into exile by the Babylonians, the prophet Habakkuk asked some difficult questions of the LORD: Why would the LORD allow wickedness to continue in Judah, and why would He use wicked people to punish Judah? His eager anticipation and expectancy of an answer from God and His submission to God's will are seen in the following verse:

---

[111] Tripp, Paul David. *New Morning Mercies: A Daily Gospel Devotional* (Wheaton, IL: Crossway, 2014), entry for March 2. **Appendix 9, Part II** is a graphical explanation of the "already" and "not yet" aspects of salvation.

I will stand on my guard post
And station myself on the rampart;
And **I will keep watch** to see what He will speak to me,
And how I may reply when I am reproved. (Habakkuk 2:1)

All ancient cities were protected by walls, and watchmen were posted atop these walls (the ramparts) throughout the night to detect any invading army (in this case, the Babylonians) and forewarn the city. On the other hand, the image of being "stationed on a rampart" could be that of a watchman waiting from atop the walls of an already besieged city for the arrival of a delivering army. In the next verses God did, indeed, answer Habakkuk, by telling him to write, wait and watch. The vision he was given was "yet for the appointed time." The land of Judah would in fact be stripped of its wealth by the Babylonians. Habakkuk "nearly collapsed"[112] because of the vision (not the one he had hoped for), but his faith remained in the LORD. His book ends in a paean of praise because God had met him in his waiting:

<u>**Though**</u> the fig tree should not blossom
And there be no fruit on the vines,
<u>**Though**</u> the yield of the olive should fail
And the fields produce no food,
<u>**Though**</u> the flock should be cut off from the fold
And there be no cattle in the stalls,
<u>**Yet**</u> **I will** exult in the Lord,
<u>**I will**</u> rejoice in the God of my salvation. (Habakkuk 3:17-18)

That's waiting. The story is told in the emboldened words above. **Even though** God allows all kinds of bad things to happen, **yet I will** trust and praise Him. Habakkuk made a definitive choice ("I

---

[112] *Ryrie Study Bible (1995),* note for Habakkuk 3:16.

will") to wait on God, despite his circumstances, a decision to continue dwelling in God. One might say he "took his soul in-hand," as discussed earlier.[113] God would indeed save a remnant in exile and return them from Babylon to their own land. Many of the promises for this restoration have yet to be fulfilled in the Millennial Kingdom because Israel was not completely ready to believe and obey God even upon their return from exile. But God was faithful to hear and respond. Isaiah foretold Babylon's destruction, again employing the image of a watchman on a wall, in Isaiah Chapter 21.[114] "Indeed, none of those who **wait** for You will be ashamed...For You I **wait** all the day...All the paths of the LORD are lovingkindness and truth / To those who keep His covenant and His testimonies" (Psalms 25:3, 5, 10). Also, "For the Scripture says, 'Whoever believes in Him will not be disappointed'" (Romans 10:11). And again, "Wait for the Lord; / Be strong and let your heart take courage; / Yes, wait for the Lord" (Psalms 27:14). Finally, another powerfully encouraging promise for those who wait:

> He gives strength to the weary,
> And to *him who* lacks might He increases power.
> **Though** youths grow weary and tired,
> And vigorous young men stumble badly,
> **Yet** <u>those who wait for the Lord</u>

---

[113] Refer to **Chapter 2.1** for more on this concept. This Book of Habakkuk, according to *The Ryrie Study Bible (1995)* "Introduction" to the Book of Habakkuk, is therefore a theodicy, a defense of God's ultimate goodness, despite His allowing evil to occur. See **Chapter 2.2** for more about theodicies.

[114] I believe a literal reestablishment of Babylon (as both a religious system and as a city located in what is modern-day Iraq) will occur in the End Times; it will shortly thereafter be destroyed, once and for all (see Revelation 17 and 18 for details). Babylon is a symbol of opposition to God, used throughout the Bible, in contrast with Jerusalem (Zion).

Will gain new strength;
They will mount up *with* wings like eagles,
They will run and not get tired,
They will walk and not become weary. (Isaiah 40:29-31)

In the Old Testament, David is found praying and watching each morning.

Heed the sound of my cry for help, my King and my God,
For to You I **pray**.
In the morning, O Lord, You will hear my voice;
In the morning I will order *my prayer* to You and *eagerly*
watch. (Psalms 5:2-3)

As New Testament believers, we are to be always in prayer. I Thessalonians 5:16-18 directs us to "pray without ceasing." I take this to mean that I should have a "running dialogue" with God throughout each day, on the back-channel of my brain. Then there must also be those extended times of more intentional and focused prayer, as when Christ prayed all night before calling His twelve apostles (Mark 3). With these extended times I confess I struggle to be consistent and find it necessary to use a list and my journal, as I explain earlier in **Chapter 2.1**. We find an incredible promise regarding focused, intentional prayer in I John 5:14-15:

This is the confidence which we have before Him, that, if we ask anything according to His will, He hears us. And if we know that He hears us *in* whatever we ask, we know that we have the requests which we have asked from Him.

If we're being honest, the perennial question asked by anyone seeking to spend regular, extended time with the LORD in focused and intentional prayer is, "How do I keep my mind from wandering?" This question brings to mind Christ's words to His weary disciples whom He had asked to "watch and pray" for Him (and for themselves as well, as they were all about to be sorely tested), just before His arrest leading to His crucifixion.

And He came to the disciples and found them sleeping, and said to Peter, "So, you *men* could not keep watch with Me for one hour? Keep watching and praying that you may not enter into temptation; **the spirit is willing, but the flesh is weak.**"

"The spirit is willing, but the flesh is weak." He gets it. He completely understands our weaknesses, how difficult it can be for us to stay focused in prayer. And He will meet us at such times when we need Him to help us pray but feel unable to do so on our own. I have found the following practical steps useful as I seek to pray in an extended, intentional and focused manner:

1. **Remind myself with Whom I'm speaking.** Now, I don't mean this in a condescending, sanctimonious way—quite the opposite. I remind myself not only of His awe-inspiring power and goodness, but also of His compassion, His concern for the people He ministered to and for those who came to Him for help, and of His accessibility and approachability (as we discussed in **Chapter 1.5**). I seek to incorporate Scripture where possible to remind me of these things. I have mentioned this earlier, but it bears repeating here: I love to use my phone to locate Scriptures. If I say the word "Bible" to my Google Assistant, and then immediately after that say the word or phrase from the Bible that flashes into my mind, I will instantly have the Scripture reference for that verse. I then use BibleGateway.com for the NASB 1995 version to get the complete verse. Again, a word of caution here: it is very easy to get sidetracked (at least for me) when using digital devices—especially while I'm praying!

2. **Use a prayer list**. I divide mine up into three sections: **People, Organizations** and **Issues**. I use different colored pens and highlighters. I try to physically place my finger on the name of the person or item I'm praying for, as it appears on the list, while I move through the list. I don't try to cover the entire list in a single session.

3. **Write out my prayers in a journal**. I directly address God using His covenant name, *LORD*, as in the NASB. More was said earlier in **Chapter 2.1** about journaling, and the example David set for us in writing many of his Psalms as direct prayers to God. (See also the end of **Chapter 5** for more discussion on this topic.) This is my preferred way of praying, and I attempt to incorporate items on my list as I journal. In fact, I keep my prayer list, my to-do list, my journal and my calendar all in the same loose-leaf notebook. Oh, and don't forget to go back and annotate the journal entry when a specific prayer has been answered!

4. **Pray out loud**. This one is the failsafe for me in being able to focus my mind. It is also the most difficult for me, and for that reason I use it the least. My mind seems to move faster and with greater fluency when I pray silently. On the other hand, if the words that pass through my mind while I'm praying silently were to be broadcast live, I'm afraid it may sound a lot like gibberish to most listeners. More on praying Scripture out loud follows below. My bottom line on this mode of prayer is that I need to be more faithful in doing more of it!

Finally, there are times when "the Spirit Himself intercedes for us with groanings too deep for words" (Romans 8:26-27):

In the same way the Spirit also helps our weakness; for we do not know how to pray as we should, but the Spirit Himself intercedes for *us* with groanings too deep for words; and He who searches the hearts knows what the mind of the Spirit is, because He intercedes for the saints according to *the will of* God.

In such times, we have only to "**be still** and know that [He] is God" (Psalms 46:10, KJV). The NASB has the words *be still* as *cease striving*. That gives a better sense that there will be times in the lives of all believers when we become so overwhelmed with life, discouragement or despair that words will simply fail to adequately express our thoughts and feelings to God. At such times, we may seek to let the Spirit direct us to passages of Scripture (for me, typically these are in the Psalms or Isaiah, as below with Isaiah 55) that express either our feelings or the answer that God may be providing to our prayer. Sometimes for me, that answer has been, "Just **wait** and trust Me on this one."

"For My thoughts are not your thoughts,
Nor are your ways My ways," declares the Lord.
"For *as* the heavens are higher than the earth,
So are My ways higher than your ways
And My thoughts than your thoughts." (Isaiah 55:8-9)

William Cowper, an eighteenth-century British poet, wrote a poem entitled "Light Shining Out of Darkness" that speaks most eloquently to this point of our not always knowing or understanding in exhaustive detail exactly what God is up to. It is attached as **Appendix 6**. You will notice that it contains the familiar line "God moves in a mysterious way, / His wonders to perform..." Cowper suffered his entire lifetime from extreme depression (known then as 'melancholy,' a condition for which no treatment was then available, as there is today), in desperation attempting suicide on more than one occasion. Despite this challenge, he persevered in his faith, producing many fine poems and hymns as a result. Additionally, a German writer named Katharina Amalia Dorothea von Schlegel wrote the hymn "**Be Still My Soul**" in 1752, later translated into English in 1855 by Jane Laurie Borthwick.[115] The lyrics of this great hymn (in **Appendix 7**) speak beautifully to this issue of God's sovereignty and providence, and of praying to and trusting Him when our impulse is to fret, worry and despair. I kept these lyrics taped beside my computer screen while I was teaching school, and since I have retired, they have been posted in my study. They represent yet another great example of what D. Martyn Lloyd-Jones referred to as "taking [one's] soul in-hand" (See **Chapter 2.1**). Psalms 131, another Psalm of Ascents written by David, also speaks beautifully to this same idea:

> Lord, my heart is not proud, nor my eyes arrogant;
> Nor do I involve myself in great matters,
> Or in things too difficult for me.
> **I have certainly soothed and quieted my soul**;
> Like a weaned child *resting* against his mother,
> My soul within me is like a weaned child.
> Israel, **wait** for the Lord
> From this time *on* and forever.

As stated above, Christ asked His disciples to **watch and pray** for Him before His crucifixion. Often in the New Testament, the word *watch*, or the concept of watching, relates to anticipating or watching for the LORD's Second Coming:

---

[115] *"Finlandia* Hymn." Wikipedia, 21 August 2020. Accessed 29 September 2020. <en.wikipedia.org/wiki/Finlandia_hymn#%22Be_still,_my_soul%22>

"Take heed, **keep on the alert**; for you do not know when the *appointed* time will come. (Mark 13:33)

Therefore, **be on the alert**—for you do not know when the master of the house is coming, whether in the evening, at midnight, or when the rooster crows, or in the morning— in case he should come suddenly and find you asleep. What I say to you I say to all, '**Be on the alert!**'" (Mark 13:35-37)

"Yes, I am coming quickly." Amen. Come, Lord Jesus. (Revelation 22:20)

Incredibly, we are never actually apart from God (Psalms 139 says, "Where can I go from your presence?"), once we have been born again; He "will never fail us or forsake us" (Hebrews 13:5) and will actually "go before us" (Deuteronomy 31:8). But our fellowship with him can be interrupted by any unconfessed sin. When we persist in sin, we "grieve" His Holy Spirit (Ephesians 4:30) within us, and we become less aware of His presence. The connection of waiting, watching and praying to dwelling should be obvious by now: We wait and watch for a fresh awareness of the LORD's presence. We wait and watch for His provision for our needs and direction for our lives. To be in His presence is to be delivered from any less-than-ideal situation we may find ourselves in because our LORD is completely sovereign in all circumstances and completely good. This will not always mean that He will rid us of the adversities we face. Paul famously prayed three times to be rid of his "thorn in the flesh," but God assured him that He was with Paul and that His power would be perfected in Paul's weakness (II Corinthians 12). The thorn in the flesh would prove to be for Paul's own benefit or good. God would provide Paul with the grace he needed to abide in his challenge. In heaven, there will be no more waiting and watching because we will be with Him, to dwell in His presence forever. Thorns will be unnecessary there. In this body of flesh, however, **prayer is our way of speaking with God**, and His primary way of speaking with us is through His Word, through His Spirit's illumination.[116]

I have not here attempted to completely examine the topic of prayer, as that has already been more than adequately accomplished by many others.[117] Our purpose here has been, rather, to note the central importance of prayer to dwelling in Christ. Philippians 4:6-7 tells us to "have no anxiety about anything, but in everything by prayer and supplication with thanksgiving, let your requests be made known to God. And the peace of God, which passes all understanding, will guard your hearts and your minds in Christ Jesus." It is this casting-off (or literally rolling off) of our burdens onto Christ that frees us to realize our true fellowship in dwelling with Him. He knows the burdens of our hearts even before we speak them (Psalms 139:4), but it is in speaking them (or writing them out in a journal) that we are freed. This is precisely the image in I Peter 5:7, which says, "...casting all your anxiety on Him because He cares for you." Once I have done this and confessed any known sin (I John 1:9), I am free to pray a Psalm to Him or to **worship** Him by meditating through some of the great lyrics of the prophets (Isaiah 40-66 is one of my favorite landing places[118]). In fact, I love to highlight

---

[116] Illumination should not be confused with interpretation. More on this will be discussed in **Chapter 6**.

[117] Andrew Murray and E.M. Bounds both produced classic works on the topic of prayer. **I have found the simple acrostic A.C.T.S. to be helpful in ordering my prayers: Adoration, Confession, Thanksgiving and Supplication. Our Lord's model prayer in Matthew 6 and Luke 12 follows this pattern.**

[118] More will be said on this point below in **Chapter 6**, but it is important to remember that, when reading the prophets, we cannot automatically take the pronoun *you*, for example, to be referring directly to us personally, without first examining it in its grammatical, historical, cultural and textual context. This is

favorite passages in my Bible and make notes as I am doing this. It is not unusual to have several dates written in beside a single passage. One such passage that has helped me to "unload" is Psalms 88. Most other "lament Psalms" begin with a complaint and end on a note of praise. Not so with this psalm. Why, then, did the Lord determine that this psalm should be included in the Psalter? The value I have found in it is that it demonstrates that the God I worship understands and cares about my burdens, regardless of how depressed I may have become over them. The psalmist voices a desperate cry for help here, directly addressing (one might even say accusing) God. He even resorts to sarcastic rhetorical questions, such as, "Can I share my faith with others from the grave?" (verses 11-12) It is further significant to me that he begins this psalm proclaiming his faith in God for salvation, and throughout the entire psalm assumes that God is completely in control of the difficult circumstances in his life. I particularly at times have identified with the statements he makes regarding his relationships, such as in verse 8:

You have removed my acquaintances far from me;
You have made me an object of loathing to them;
I am shut up and cannot go out.

---

particularly important in reading the prophets. For example, Jerimiah 29:11 says, "I know the plans I have for you, plans for good and not for evil, to give you a future and a hope." The *you* in this verse was the Southern Kingdom of Judah that was about to be taken into captivity, and few would live to see it end in seventy years. I believe, however, that we have been grafted in to the promises of Israel (Romans 9-11, Ephesians 1-2) and that that same heart of God is now extended to His followers today; so, I am able to claim this verse in application to my own life, understanding that the "good" as the word is used in Romans 8:28 may not always be the exact wishes I have in mind.

I'm not sure what, if anything, this psalmist did to merit such treatment, but I'm actually glad it isn't stated. In that way it becomes more universally applicable to situations I might face.

Two final points on prayer warrant emphasis here. I have perhaps saved them for last because they are the weakest links in my own personal prayer life, and the ones I feel the least qualified to write about. I am referring here to praise and fasting as elements of prayer that please God and accomplish His work in our lives as we pray. First, **praise** is essentially acknowledging God for Who He is, while thanksgiving is acknowledging Him for what He has done. These terms are often confused—and I don't suppose it really matters to God, as long as we practice both—but true praise to God for Who He is I find often lacking in the prayers of His saints. I am always impressed in the masterful way that my wife Sara offers praise to God when she prays. She names His attributes (especially for His faithfulness and lovingkindness) and reminds Him of, and thanks Him for, His specific promises that bear upon the issues we are praying about. One has only to read through the Psalms (particularly those near the end of the Psalter) to gain an appreciation for how important praise is to God and to us as we pray. I am endeavoring to use the Psalms more often as I seek to rehabilitate my prayer life in this area.

Secondly, **fasting** is a discipline that we see practiced in both the Old and New Testaments, despite the fact that it is never commanded for New Testament followers of Christ. It is, however, always mentioned in association with prayer. Jesus instructed His disciples,

> Whenever you fast, do not put on a gloomy face as the hypocrites *do*, for they neglect their appearance so that they will be noticed by men when they are fasting. Truly I say to

you, they have their reward in full. But you, when you fast, anoint your head and wash your face so that your fasting will not be noticed by men, but by your Father who is in secret; and your Father who sees *what is done* in secret will reward you. (Matthew 6:16-18)

Fasting is therefore to be done "in secret" (or privately), and Jesus did not say, "**If** you fast..." but rather "**whenever** you fast...." That is, He assumed His disciples would fast, as He, Himself did. The practice of fasting should always be undertaken subject to counsel of sound medical advice, particularly in the case of those with known medical conditions, such as diabetes. I find no mention in the Scriptures of fasting from anything besides food, but I believe it is Biblical (particularly as it may relate to our earlier discussion on idols) to honor God and to deepen our relationship with Him by abstaining, from time to time, from other things such as media (in particular, social media). In the Scriptures the purpose of fasting seems to always be to purify one's soul in humility before God and to clear and refocus one's attention upon Him.

In reading Jesus' rebukes of the Pharisees in the New Testament, do you get the idea that God hates insincere, religious ostentation? When I read an Old Testament passage such as Isaiah 58, that is the same impression I come away with there. As we read it earlier in **Chapter 2.2**, where God is speaking and excoriating His own Israelite chosen ones for their lack of true humility and sincerity in their religious practices, such as fasting, He proclaims,

Is this not the fast which I choose,
To loosen the bonds of wickedness,
To undo the bands of the yoke,
And to let the oppressed go free
And break every yoke?

Is it not to divide your bread with the hungry
And bring the homeless poor into the house;
When you see the naked, to cover him...?
And not to hide yourself from your own flesh? (Isaiah 58:6-7)

So, done in secret and in true humility to honor God, and demonstrating love for those who are needy around us, fasting can help us to refocus upon God. That's the purpose, process and outcome of Biblical fasting.

One of the most compelling stories of answered prayer I know of is that of Hezekiah, king of Judah, when his capitol city of Jerusalem was surrounded by 185,000 vicious Assyrian soldiers, known and feared for their cruelty, all intent on conquering the city (as detailed in II Kings 19 and Isaiah 37). The attackers send a letter to King Hezekiah detailing their threats and insulting the God of Judah. King Hezekiah takes the letter to the temple and spreads it out before the LORD. I love this image because it speaks to what I often do in "spreading out my own problems before the Lord." In **waiting** for the LORD there, Hezekiah pours out his soul in **prayer** (in verses 14 through 19 of II Kings 19). Isaiah the prophet then comes to him and announces that God has heard Hezekiah's prayer. The following morning the **watchmen on the walls** see 185,000 Assyrian corpses strewn about the countryside surrounding Jerusalem. The Assyrian king has been called away, back to his capitol city, where he is slain by political rivals. In celebration of this dramatic deliverance and rescue, an unknown author wrote Psalms 46, which contains the powerful words of **praise** and **worship** below:

God is our refuge and strength,

A very present help in trouble.
Therefore we will not fear, though the earth should change
And though the mountains slip into the heart of the sea....

"*Cease striving* [or "be still"] and know that I am God;
I will be exalted among the nations, I will be exalted in the
earth."
The Lord of hosts is with us;
The God of Jacob is our stronghold.

Worship of God is often thought to be simply the singing of
hymns of praise to God in corporate worship services, and we call
the person who leads such music our *Worship Leader.* Our own
Worship Leader, however, frequently incorporates Scripture
reading and a personal reflection on the passage read prior to the
singing of the actual music, and the songs he selects carefully
correlate with the message the Pastor delivers. I would offer as a
definition of worship the following: Active and complete
engagement of our minds, our emotions and our wills, expressed
through our words/voices and actions in acknowledgment of and
total submission to the truth about God and His will for us as
found in His Word. Jesus told us that we should Worship God in
both spirit and in truth:

God is spirit, and those who worship Him must worship in
spirit and truth. (John 4:24)

Thus, there is both a subjective and an objective element in true
worship.

By this definition, every act we perform (even our daily work) may
therefore become an act of worship, if done as unto God:

> **Whatever you do,** do your work heartily, as for the Lord
> rather than for men, knowing that from the Lord you will
> receive the reward of the inheritance. **It is the Lord Christ
> whom you serve.** (Colossians 3:23-24)

This is not to suggest that worship should not be incorporated into our daily personal devotional time with the LORD. I believe that it definitely should be, as evidenced by Jesus' words from John 4:24 above. Also, this is not in any way to minimize the importance of corporate worship—in fact, we are **commanded** to join in corporate worship (see for example, Hebrews 10:24-25). Many of the Psalms were written for this very purpose, to be recited or sung to the Lord in a corporate setting. Psalms 42:5 states,

> These things I remember and I pour out my soul within me.
> For I used to go along with the throng *and* lead them in
> procession to the house of God,
> With the voice of joy and thanksgiving, a multitude keeping
> festival.

So, let us then wait, watch, pray, fast and worship as those who dwell in Christ's stronghold. He speaks to us through His Word (as He did to Hezekiah through His prophet Isaiah), and we may speak to Him through our prayers and our worship.

For Further Thought:

1. What does it mean to wait on God?

2. What am I waiting on God for right now?

3. Isaiah 64:5 says that God "acts in behalf of the one who waits for Him." What other promises are given to those who wait on the LORD?

4. How might praying involve the use of Scripture? The use of a journal? The use of a prayer list?

5. How often do I pray out loud to God in my private time with Him? Have I ever used a worship song in my private time with the LORD?

6. What kinds of issues could keep us from praying, and how might we overcome these?

7. How should we respond when God doesn't seem to be answering our prayers? How is it possible for us to pray even when we don't feel as if we are able to do so?

8. How might I incorporate worship into my daily devotional time with the Lord? When was the last time I sang a song of praise to God during my private devotional time?

9. How are waiting, watching, praying and worshiping related to dwelling?

Chapter 5

Rest

Come to Me, all who are weary and heavy-laden, and I will give you rest. (Matthew 11:28)

Early on, in the very beginning, our God established how He thought about rest. He modeled the concept for us, Himself, just so that we wouldn't miss it.

> By the seventh day God completed His work which He had done, and He rested on the seventh day from all His work which He had done. Then God blessed the seventh day and sanctified it, because in it He rested from all His work which God had created and made. (Genesis 2:2-3)

Later, in Leviticus (with seven being the number of perfection), He gave laws concerning the Sabbath (seventh) Day (**Chapter 23**), the Sabbath (seventh) Year (**Chapter 25**) and the Jubilee Year (seven times seven equals forty-nine years—so, every fiftieth year).

You are also to count off seven sabbaths of years for yourself, seven times seven years, so that you have the time of the seven sabbaths of years, namely, forty-nine years. You shall then sound a ram's horn abroad on the tenth day of the seventh month; on the day of atonement you shall sound a horn all through your land. You shall thus consecrate the fiftieth year and proclaim a release through the land to all its inhabitants. It shall be a jubilee for you, and each of you shall return to his own property, and each of you shall return to his family. You shall have the fiftieth year as a jubilee; you shall not sow, nor reap its aftergrowth, nor gather in from its untrimmed vines. For it is a jubilee; it shall be holy to you. You shall eat its crops out of the field. "On this year of jubilee each of you shall return to his own property." (Leviticus 25:8-13)

Thus, He established a healthy rhythm between work and rest, lest the people He had created make an idol out of their work and their accumulation of wealth. (And in case you missed it, wealth or property must be returned to its original owners!) That same expectation of periodic rest, a redirection of focus away from stress in the accumulation of wealth and a focus on family and social unity is carried over into the New Testament. The verse quoted above, Matthew 11:28, is probably the lodestar New Testament verse on rest, and Matthew 11:28-30 is a defining passage on the accessibility and approachability of Christ, as we discussed earlier in the section by that title in **Chapter 1.5**:

Come to Me, all who are weary and heavy-laden, and I will give you rest. Take My yoke upon you and learn from Me, for I am gentle and humble in heart, and you will find rest for your souls. For My yoke is easy and My burden is light. (Matthew 11:28-30)

Even though I am retired, simply when I think about my multipage to-do list, and the deadlines and appointments that fill up my weeks, I frequently find myself overwhelmed, experiencing anything but rest. I have found rest to be a discipline I have to learn from the Holy Spirit, to be able to live in "day-tight increments," as discussed in **Chapter 2.3** and Matthew 6:33-34. In addition, Hebrews 4 is more or less a defining chapter on the Biblical concept of resting. The word *rest* (or one of its derivatives) is used fourteen times (plus three additional times in Chapter 3). In this passage (3:7-4:11) *rest* may refer to any of the following, depending upon the context:

1. Israel's rest from wandering in the wilderness as they entered the Promised Land

2. God's Sabbath rest in creation

3. Our rest from works in attempting to earn salvation

4. Our rest in the sanctification process as we rely on His power at work within us

5. Our future rest in the Millennium and the New Earth

Wherever the Old Testament is quoted in this passage, the reference is generally to the first item above. Verses 4:8-11a make clear, however, that the **rest** being referred to is extended to other meanings:

> For if Joshua had given them **rest,** He would not have spoken of another day after that. So there remains a Sabbath **rest** for the people of God. For the one who has entered His **rest** has

himself also **rested** from his works, as God did from His. Therefore, let us be diligent to enter that **rest**....[119]

I believe the writer of Hebrews has in mind the concept of *shalom* in referring to items 2-5 above. In ancient Hebrew, the word denotes "peace, harmony, wholeness, completeness, prosperity, welfare and tranquility."[120] The prophet Isaiah, in Chapter 26, is providing the lyrics of a song that will be sung in the land of Judah "in that day" (the day of the Millennium). In verse 3 the lyrics read "The steadfast of mind (or in the RSV, 'him...whose mind is stayed on Thee') You will keep in **perfect peace [shalom]** / Because he trusts in You." This concept of trusting in God to provide what we are unable to provide for ourselves was touched on earlier in our discussion on prayer, as in (literally) casting or rolling our burdens upon Him. In verse 9, Isaiah says, "At night my soul longs for you / Indeed, my spirit within me seeks You diligently...." Verse 12 continues, "Lord, You will establish **peace** for us / Since You have also performed for us all our works." So in the Millennium, as I put this together, we will **rest in perfect peace** as we commune with (**dwell** with) our LORD. Works to earn salvation or to become more like Him through the sanctification process will be unnecessary. "Beloved, now we are children of God, and it has not appeared as yet what we will be. We know that when He appears, we will be like Him, because we will see Him just as He is" (I John 3:2). That will be true **rest**, true **peace**, indeed. But how might that **rest** be a reality in our lives today? Answer:

---

[119] Note the paradox in being diligent to rest. This underscores the fact that we must respond to the grace of God with obedience, while avoiding legalism.

[120] From *Wikipedia*, "Shalom," 6 June 2020. <https://en.wikipedia.org/wiki/Shalom>.

We must "take our souls in-hand"[121] and call to mind (to correlate with the list above) the realities that:

1. "...there remains a Sabbath rest for the people of God" (Hebrews 4:9).

2. "[We] are looking forward to the city...whose builder and maker is God" (Hebrews 11:10).

3. "He saved us, not on the basis of deeds which we have done in righteousness, but according to His mercy, by the washing of regeneration and renewing by the Holy Spirit, whom He poured out upon us richly through Jesus Christ our Savior" (Titus 3:5-6).

4. "[He] is able to do far more abundantly beyond all that we ask or think, according to the power that works within us" (Ephesians 3:20).

5. We have a great hope in His return: "But we do not want you to be uninformed, brethren, about those who are asleep, so that you will not grieve as do the rest who have no hope. For if we believe that Jesus died and rose again, even so God will bring with Him those who have fallen asleep in Jesus. For this we say to you by the word of the Lord, that we who are alive and remain until the coming of the Lord, will not precede those who have fallen asleep. For the Lord Himself will descend from heaven with a shout, with the voice of *the* archangel and with the trumpet of God, and the dead in Christ will rise first. Then we who are alive and remain will be caught up together with them in the clouds to meet the Lord in the

---

[121] Refer back to **Chapter 2.1** for more on the concept of "taking our souls in-hand."

air, and so we shall always be with the Lord. Therefore comfort one another with these words" (I Thessalonians 4:13-18).

In these things we can rejoice at the present time, as we dwell in Christ. Psalms 23 is a most beautiful picture of this rest and *shalom* that our LORD offers us. Notice that this peace occurs even "...in the presence of my enemies" (verse 5). As stated above, Jesus instructed, "Come to Me, all who are weary and heavy-laden, and I will give you **rest**. Take My yoke upon you and learn from Me, for **I am gentle and humble in heart**, and you will find **rest for your souls**. For My yoke is easy and My burden is light" (Matthew 11:28-30). Philippians 4 is a wonderful statement of this **peace** found in the Christian life. This is a **peace/rest** that knows the "secret" of contentment "in any and every circumstance" (verses 11-12). It "rejoice[s] always," is "anxious for nothing" but "let[s] [its] requests be made known to God" (verse 6), and directs [its] mind to "**dwell** on…things" that are true, honorable, right, pure, lovely, of good repute, excellent and praise-worthy (verse 8). These are directions (imperative mood verbs), as well as promises. That takes us back to our earlier discussion on how **dwelling** is a reciprocal activity[122]—we obey, and God will fulfill His promises, but He begins the whole process by being unconditionally with us in all circumstances. All of our obedience follows in response to that amazing truth. In military close-order drill, there is a command of "Parade Rest," which, when properly executed, is anything but restful. The same principle applies here. Paradoxically, we are **commanded** to rest,[123] however, here we are met with the "easy yoke" and the "light burden" and the gentleness

---

[122] See **Chapter 2.1**, "A Seeming Paradox."

[123] "Rest in the Lord and wait patiently for Him…" (Psalms 37:7).

and humility of a Savior who makes true **rest** for our souls possible.

Before we leave this important topic of rest, let us reexamine more closely the rest Christ offers us in the sanctification process (point 4 above). This is where we must realistically seek to address the questions raised by those who would say, "Okay, I try to obey, but I keep committing the same sin over and over again. I know I must have disqualified myself from dwelling with Christ; so, I can't think why He would still be wanting to dwell with me!" You may recall from our previous discussion on legalism as a "Hindrance to Dwelling" in **Chapter 1.3**, we saw that God is not so much interested in a perfect (legal) track record in our obeying Him (in fact, that would be impossible!) as He is in where our hearts are at any given time.[124] We saw that true dwelling with Christ is predicated upon neither ritual nor routine, but rather upon relationship—where are we at any given time with our heart relationship with Christ? If we keep our hearts in the right place, then obedience will follow. The Scriptures say, "Watch over [guard] your heart with all diligence, / For from it *flow* the springs of life" (Proverbs 4:23). So practically speaking, how do we keep our hearts right? I can share how I seek to achieve this in the hopes it may be of some benefit. I typically try to use a four-step method,[125] remembering that the power is not in the method itself, but in our relationship with our very present God (Psalms 46):

1. Pour my heart out in repentance and supplication before the LORD as described in **Chapter 4** on prayer. This always involves my use of a journal in which I directly address the

---

[124] **Appendix 9, Part II** provides a graphical explanation of the term *heart*.

[125] Some readers may notice the similarities that exist between this and the various twelve-step recovery programs out there today (initially developed by Alcoholics Anonymous).

125

LORD in writing out my prayer. This may seem awkward at first, but it will soon become a welcome way of unloading, reconnecting and remembering.

2. Find in the Psalms, one that directly states how I feel about my failure and my desire to dwell with Christ, and pray this psalm out loud to Him as often as necessary.[126] (Psalms 51 is a favorite go-to of mine.) I would suggest writing the date in your Bible beside the passage that speaks to your heart. There are many great "lament" and "penitential" (repenting or confessional) psalms that are perfect for this purpose.

3. In my journal, I write out a practical plan to remove any sin from my life. This might include such pragmatic steps as withdrawing from a detrimental activity or relationship, destroying anything that would be sinful or addictive, and being willing to seek forgiveness from someone I may have wrongfully offended, where possible and appropriate and as directed by the LORD (Matthew 5:23-24).[127] This might involve first seeking counsel from a godly, trusted friend; or better, from a spouse.

4. Find a fellow believer with whom I can share what I am doing, and become accountable to that person. Ask this person to pray for me. As above, this is most ideally done with a spouse.

---

[126] An excellent new resource to use for this purpose is David Jerimiah's book *Shelter in God: Your Refuge in Times of Trouble* (Nashville: Thomas Nelson, 2020). This is an encouraging explication of ten selected psalms related to the idea of seeking refuge.

[127] I would always seek first to ask myself, "Could this attempt at reconciliation be done in a way that would genuinely benefit the person offended, or would it simply be a way for me to seek to assuage my own conscience?"

The net effect of the above actions is to restore rest to my soul as I dwell with Christ. Some of David's closest times with his LORD were the times when he found himself at the end of his wits, in utter distress and despair, sometimes because of some mistake he had made. In these times he cried out and found God always ready to meet him with forgiveness, restoration and rest.[128] This is not to say there were never consequences for his sins, just that God used those consequences to refine David's character even further. Remember, when Jesus was asked what the most important commandment was, he did not respond "**Obey** the LORD," but rather "**Love** the LORD with all your heart" (Matthew 22:37) because he knew that the one who loved the LORD would be the same one who also obeyed the LORD ("He who has my commandments and keeps them, he it is who loves me" [John 14:21]). Finding rest must always begin with this relationship we have with Christ. It cannot be overemphasized—dwelling with Christ is not about legalistic ritual or routine; it is about relationship! This I have learned the hard way.

There are also times of genuine discouragement in the lives of believers that aren't specifically related to sin in our lives. They are simply the results of circumstances beyond our control. For one such example, David found himself hiding in a cave from King Saul, who was pursuing him (in I Samuel 22). Saul was jealous of David and intent on killing him. When the word spread that David was in the cave, he was joined by 400 other refugees, who were themselves all in need of deliverance by David from some need or another. In the midst of this desperate situation David pours out his soul to the LORD in Psalms 142:

---

[128] Read the account of David's sin with Bathsheba and Uriah and his restored relationship with God in II Samuel 11.

I cry aloud with my voice to the Lord;
I make supplication with my voice to the Lord.
² I pour out my complaint before Him;
I declare my trouble before Him.
³ When my spirit was overwhelmed within me,
You knew my path.
In the way where I walk
They have hidden a trap for me.
⁴ Look to the right and see;
For there is no one who regards me;

There is no escape for me;
No one cares for my soul.

⁵ I cried out to You, O Lord;
I said, "You are my refuge,
My portion in the land of the living.
⁶ "Give heed to my cry,
For I am brought very low;
Deliver me from my persecutors,
For they are too strong for me.
⁷ "Bring my soul out of prison,
So that I may give thanks to Your name;
The righteous will surround me,
For You will deal bountifully with me."

David Jeremiah points out that David felt discouraged, disoriented, deserted, depressed and defeated.[129] Three times he "cries out to God" (verses 1, 5 and 6) for help. **But don't fail to notice this—David was writing this all down! His "journal" became this psalm in our Bibles.**

---

[129] Jeremiah, pp. 164-172.

We should begin to realize the value of keeping our own journals. I feel very strongly about that particular discipline. I hope you're taking time to regularly record your thoughts and prayers before God.... David went beyond simple journaling. He went beyond simply recording for us the events of his life. **He wrote out his prayers to God**, then kept an account of God's workings. Here in our Bibles we can actually chart the course of David's life as he moves through his series of crises and emerges victorious on the other side.[130] [emphasis added]

As David Jeremiah further points out, within this psalm, David (1) verbalizes his problems to God, (2) recognizes his presence before God, (3) realizes his provision in God and (4) resumes his praise to God.[131] That should sound familiar because it is very close to the four-step process outlined above—God meets us where we are, reveals Himself as our deliverer, and then carries us forward out of despair. That is how we regain rest, through pouring out our hearts before God and then clinging to His promises. By that scenario, it would be impossible to realize true rest without being actively engaged with Scripture, which is the topic of our next chapter.

For Further Thought:

1. How is it possible to unburden our souls and find true rest?

2. What could prevent or hinder us from finding this rest? How might we overcome these things and regain true rest?

---

[130] Ibid., p. 162.
[131] Ibid., pp. 172-177.

3. How would you respond to someone who would say, "God doesn't want me to rest; He wants me to serve"? Are resting and serving mutually exclusive?

4. How is rest hindered by legalism? (Hint: Reexamine the context of Matthew 11:28-30)

5. How is rest related to dwelling?

6. How should the principle of a Sabbath rest be applied in your own life? Is there a healthy rhythm of work and rest/worship in your own life and family?

7. How is it possible to unburden our hearts and find true deliverance, forgiveness and rest from our genuine guilt from habitual sin?

Chapter 6

Study and Meditate—Going Beyond Mere Casual Reading

O how I love Your law! / It is my meditation all the day.
(Psalms 119:97)

Your word is a lamp to my feet / And a light to my path.
(Psalms 119:105)

The Christian who would actively dwell with Christ must be one who is devoted to study of and meditation on His Word. II Timothy 2:15 directs such a one to "**be diligent** to present yourself approved to God as a workman who does not need to be ashamed, accurately handling the word of truth." The words *be diligent* are translated as **study** in the KJV. In the Old Testament, as he assumed his leadership role from Moses, Joshua was commanded by God, "This book of the law shall not depart from your mouth, but you shall **meditate** on it day and night, so that you may be careful to do according to all that is written in it; for then you will make your way prosperous, and then you will have success" (Joshua 1:8). David wrote in Psalms 1 that a Godly man is one who has his delight "in the law of the Lord, and in His law he **meditates** all the day." Psalms 119, the longest chapter in the Bible, is devoted entirely to the topic of the psalmist's delight in the Word of God. Psalms 4:4 gives us, "Tremble, and do not sin; / Meditate in your heart upon your bed, and be still." Jeremiah proclaimed, "Your words were found and I ate them, / And Your words became for me a joy and the delight of my heart; / For I have been called by Your name, / O Lord God of hosts" (Jeremiah 15:16). The man or woman who would **dwell** with Christ must be one who methodically studies, and continually meditates on, the Word of God. So, what does it mean to study and meditate on Scripture?

It would be fair to say that most Christians would, ideally, seek to be in the Scriptures daily. Many use a daily devotional guide such as *Open Windows* or (my personal favorites) *Today in the Word* from Moody Bible Institute, and *New Morning Mercies: A Daily Gospel Devotional*, by Paul David Tripp (Wheaton, IL: Crossway, 2014). Others seek to then also systematically read through their entire Bibles. I have found that these plans work best when a simple checklist is used, listing each chapter of each book of the Bible—instead of one that tries to get through the Bible within a single year. They also work best using a study Bible that answers questions that will assuredly arise while reading. My personal favorites are the MacArthur and Ryrie Study Bibles in the NASB (1995) version. These particular study Bibles are doctrinally sound, as must be determined for whichever one you may select. If the simple checklist is used, one could still get through the Bible within a year, but one should not get discouraged if he or she fell behind at some point. Some Christians rely solely on hearing the Bible taught on Sunday, or on a favorite Bible radio program or podcast, which is inadequate in view of the fact that we retain less of what we merely hear as time passes. I have found that digital delivery of a daily devotional is often distracting—too easy for me to get sidetracked into email, text messaging or social media. Also, online forums on Bible verses of the day can easily become sources of misinformation. The Navigators developed a famous illustration many years ago called "The Hand Illustration" to explain how meditation is used with each of four methods of intake for God's Word: hearing, reading, studying and memorizing. The "thumb" in their metaphor, which must be used in conjunction with the "fingers" in order to "hold onto" the Word, is meditation. Each of the remaining fingers is a different method of intake. The more fingers used, the better the grip or hold. It becomes easy to see how hearing alone (the little finger) is insufficient if someone tries to snatch the Bible from your hand, and that is precisely the purpose of our Enemy, as seen in the following passage:

> When a large crowd was coming together, and those from the various cities were journeying to Him, He spoke by way of a parable: "The sower went out to sow his seed; and as he sowed, some fell beside the road, and it was trampled under foot and the birds of the air ate it up. Other *seed* fell on rocky *soil*, and as soon as it grew up, it withered away, because it had no moisture. Other *seed* fell among the thorns; and the thorns grew up with it and choked it out. Other *seed* fell into the good soil, and grew up, and produced a crop a hundred times as great." As He said these things, He would call out, "He who has ears to hear, let him hear…. Now the parable is this: the seed is the word of God. Those beside the road are **those who have heard; then the devil comes and takes away the word from their heart,** so that they will not believe and be saved. Those on the rocky *soil are* those who, when they hear, receive the word with joy; and these have no *firm* root; they believe for a

while, and in time of temptation fall away. The *seed* which fell among the thorns, these are the ones who have heard, and as they go on their way they are choked with worries and riches and pleasures of *this* life, and bring no fruit to maturity. **But the *seed* in the good soil, these are the ones who have heard the word in an honest and good heart, and hold it fast, and bear fruit with perseverance."** (Luke 8:4-15) [emphasis added]

A 2019 study by the Barna organization revealed the current Bible-reading habits of adult Americans:[132]

- **5% are Bible Centered**: Interact with the Bible frequently. It is transforming their relationships and shaping their choices.

- **19% are Bible Engaged**: Interact with the Bible consistently. It is transforming their relationship with God and others.

- **19% are Bible Friendly**: Interact with the Bible consistently. It may be a source of spiritual insight and wisdom.

- **9% are Bible Neutral**: Interact with the Bible sporadically. It has little spiritual influence, but that influence may be growing.

- **48% are Bible Disengaged**: Interact with the Bible infrequently, if at all. It has minimal impact on their lives.

While the trend from the previous year is generally negative, I had expected the numbers to be worse. In fact, fewer Americans are

---

[132]Includes those who self-identified as non-Christians. Barna Group, "State of the Bible 2019: Trends in Engagement," April 18, 2019. Accessed December 18, 2020. <barna.com/research/state-of-the-bible-2019/>

disengaged. The obvious question remains, however: What may be done to increase the hunger for, and the effort for, serious Bible reading and Bible study among the followers of Christ? I believe the Bible can be its own magnet, drawing people through the Holy Spirit into the depths of its riches as they begin to sample the Scriptures for themselves. **What's needed is to present them with a practical approach to go beyond a superficial handling of the text.** What often passes for "Bible study" in many Evangelical churches today is making a hastily-drawn application from a casual reading of a short passage…or worse, from reading **about** a passage from a Sunday school quarterly and then making the application suggested therein, all done without spending serious time in the passage itself. Much space in the quarterlies is often devoted to extra-Biblical illustrations around the central theme touched on in the passage, all just to get the reader interested enough to read the entire lesson. Ideally, Bible study could be said to involve four steps: observation, correlation,[133] interpretation and application. Some Sunday school quarterlies in current use employ these four steps better than others. Some quarterlies are each focused upon a particular book of the Bible, while others are focused upon a particular topic. I believe I could make a stronger case for the former, much as expository preaching (that is, systematically going through one book of the Bible at a time) lends itself to a more thorough examination and exposition of the text.

---

[133] Some would include correlation—checking other passages in the Bible that relate to the one being studied—in interpretation. Howard and William Hendricks do this. I think correlation is important enough to list separately. As I read a passage, other passages will frequently jump into my mind as a word or phrase that I remember. To locate the verse(s) in the Bible, I merely say the word *Bible* to my Google Assistant, and then say the word or phrase itself. Instantly I am able to see the word or phrase in the Bible. This is in effect a virtual word (or topic) concordance. BibleGateway.org functions in the same way, allowing one to select the Bible translation preferred or to compare different translations of the same verse(s).

Arguably, the best available resource for anyone interested in learning how to study the Bible for himself or herself in a similar way (and to lead small group discussions of it) is the classic book by Howard Hendricks and his son Bill, *Living by the Book*.[134] This book is written for a lay person to understand, and provides an easy-to-apply method for moving through these four steps:

1. Observation: What does the text say?

2. Correlation: What other passages address the same topic (or contain the same word or phrase)?

3. Interpretation: What does it mean (in the mind of the original author, in its historical, cultural and grammatical context)?

4. Application: What does it mean **for me**?

There are many excellent Bible studies out there that do employ each of these four steps. These are generally published as separate fill-in-the-blanks booklets for each book of the Bible, and some are focused upon a particular topic. As with Bible commentaries and study Bibles, it is necessary to ensure that the theology of the author is sound. The Hendrickses' book gives you, the reader, the knowledge necessary to do all of this on your own.

1. **Observation**. Howard and Bill Hendricks come up with a list of six things to look for when reading a passage: Things that are emphasized, repeated, related, alike, unlike and true to life.

---

[134] Hendricks, Howard D. and William G. *Living by the Book*, Second Edition (Chicago, IL: Moody Publishers, 2007). Howard "Prof" Hendricks is estimated to have taught more than 30,000 students in his sixty years at Dallas Theological Seminary. He passed away in 2016.

There are other, more detailed lists out there,[135] but it is important here to note that we are not yet looking for an application, merely observing what is in the passage being read. There is a well-known story that illustrates the importance of this step, known as "The Student, the Fish and Agassiz." A student goes to university to study under a famous scientist, Agassiz. The student is dismayed that the professor first asks him to sit for days staring at a preserved fish specimen, until at last the student begins noticing all manner of important details.[136] We are not asked to study a dead fish, but to read a text and observe, but the same principles apply. The point is that we must discipline and train ourselves, our **minds**, how to look. Additionally, there is the issue of the general decline in serious, critical reading skills as an indication that more and more people in our culture today are becoming mentally lazy, content to be spoon-fed the quick, easy, superficial and most often wrong answers to life's questions from the media, in place of reading and thinking for themselves. This is reflected in the fact that the reading habits of Americans have changed dramatically over the last three decades. There has been a steady decline in the amount of time devoted to reading, particularly "serious reading." Phillip Yancey, a noted author and past Editor of *Christianity Today*, has commented on the distracting effect of digital media on the time he spends reading:

---

[135] The best source I have found for such a checklist is Oletta Wald's *The New Joy of Discovery in Bible Study*, published in 2002 by Augsburg Fortress (Minneapolis). See pages 17-18.

[136] From *American Poems*, Third Edition (Boston: Houghton, Osgood and Co., 1879), pp. 450-454. This essay first appeared in *Every Saturday*, XVI (Apr. 4, 1874), 369-70, under the title "In the Laboratory with Agassiz, By a former pupil." <skidmore.edu/~mmarx/L&EF09/agassiz.pdf>.

The Internet and social media have trained my brain to read a paragraph or two, and then start looking around. When I read an online article from *The Atlantic* or *The New Yorker*, after a few paragraphs I glance over at the slide bar to judge the article's length. My mind strays, and I find myself clicking on the sidebars and the underlined links. Soon I'm over at CNN.com reading Donald Trump's latest tweets and details of the latest terrorist attack, or perhaps checking tomorrow's weather. Worse, I fall prey to the little boxes that tell me, "If you like this article [or book], you'll also like…" Or I glance at the bottom of the screen and scan the teasers for more engaging tidbits: 30 Amish Facts That'll Make Your Skin Crawl; Top 10 Celebrity Wardrobe Malfunctions; Walmart Cameras Captured These Hilarious Photos. A dozen or more clicks later I have lost interest in the original article. Neuroscientists have an explanation for this phenomenon. When we learn something quick and new, we get a dopamine rush; functional-MRI brain scans show the brain's pleasure centers lighting up.[137]

This digital distraction can be, therefore, a great hindrance to dwelling, as discussed earlier in **Chapter 1.3's** "busyness." This makes sustained, serious reading (and observation) difficult, and hinders Bible study. There is much that may still be said in favor of good, old-fashioned, hard-copy books and periodicals.

---

[137] Yancey, Phillip, writing in an Op-Ed piece for *The Washington Post* entitled **"The death of reading is threatening the soul,"** July 21, 2017. Accessed July 16, 2020. <u>washingtonpost.com/news/acts-of-faith/wp/2017/07/21/the-death-of-reading-is-threatening-the-soul/</u>>

2. **Correlation.** This step involves locating other verses that contain the same thought or word, and therefore fit the passage focused upon into the context of the entire Bible. This is done to provide additional insight for interpretation, and to check for errors in interpretation. It can be accomplished through the use of a good concordance. As mentioned earlier, it is possible to utilize a Google search as a virtual concordance by typing or saying the word *"Bible"* and then the word or phrase one is looking for into a smartphone, but this does require strong discipline to avoid distraction.

3. **Interpretation.** Howard and William Hendricks explain it best:

> But if we're to have any hope of interpreting God's Word accurately, we've got to start with a fundamental premise: "Meaning" is not our subjective thoughts read into the text [that would be *eisegesis*] but God's objective truth read out of the text [that is *exegesis*]. As someone has well said, the task of Bible study is to think God's thoughts after Him. He has a Mind and He has revealed it in His Word. The miracle is that He used human authors to do so. Working through their personalities, their circumstances and their concerns, the Holy Spirit superintended the crafting of a document. And each of the human authors—God's coauthors we might call them—had a specific message in mind as he recorded his specific portion of the text. That's why I like to refer to the step of interpretation as the re-creation process. We're attempting to stand in the author's shoes and re-create his experience—to think as he thought, to feel as he felt, and to decide as he has decided. We're asking, "What did this

mean to him?" before we ever ask, "What does it mean to us?" (Hendricks 201)

The Hendrickses identify several "barriers" to interpretation, among them language (for example, identifying figures of speech such as hyperbole and idioms), culture, literary structure (for example, is it law, poetry, narrative, discourse or apocalyptic vision?) and geography. To these I would add history (we need to know in general terms the history of the ancient near-eastern world and the timeline of the Bible as it relates to this history). There are certain principles for understanding each type of literature. They go on to describe the types of tools available to overcome such barriers, including Bible dictionaries, commentaries[138] and historical atlases. (These resources are often partially available in a good study Bible.) Their Five Keys to Interpretation include content, context, comparison, culture and consultation. I can generally know I'm in trouble when I begin explaining my interpretation with the words "I think." What often follows those words is a hastily-drawn application from a first-impression interpretation. Remember, it really doesn't matter what any of us might "think" about a particular passage; the real meaning is what the original author intended it to be (**"authorial intent"** in the original language).[139] There is,

---

[138] When selecting a commentary (or study Bible), it is important to ensure the underlying theology is Biblically sound. I would highly recommend *The Moody Bible Commentary* (Chicago: Moody Press, 2014). Also, the book-by-book commentaries of John MacArthur and Warren Wiersbe are excellent.

[139] Authorial intent is the "Holy Grail" of Bible study. I cannot overstate how important this is in view of current prevailing thought in academia that any given text (Biblical or otherwise) has only the meaning assigned to it by the reader. They would argue that the text is actually created in the mind of the reader at the time it is read. The authorial intent is therefore irrelevant in this view. This argument is of course self-defeating by the very words they use to

therefore, only one true interpretation of all Scripture;[140] although, we all may err in varying degrees from ever completely understanding it, since we don't have the authors themselves here to explain (until, that is, we see the Lord, or the authors themselves, face-to-face in the afterlife). It could even be said that the original authors were sometimes at a loss themselves as to the full meaning of their own writings, as seen in the following passage:

> As to this salvation, the prophets who prophesied of the grace that *would come* to you made careful searches and inquiries, seeking to know what person or time the Spirit of Christ within them was indicating as He predicted the sufferings of Christ and the glories to follow. It was revealed to them that they were not serving themselves, but you, in these things which now have been announced to you through those who preached the gospel to you by the Holy Spirit sent from heaven—things into which angels long to look. (I Peter 1:10-12)

---

express it. The academic discipline concerned with interpretation of a text is known as *hermeneutics*. As a minimum, I have found it helpful to use a good study Bible, such as the MacArthur or Ryrie Study Bibles, in reading my Bible. It is very important to ensure that the author of the commentary in such Bibles has sound theology, or more harm may be done than good. I have noticed that, in many instances, the authors of the notes in these study Bibles will offer several possible interpretations of a given text, and then proceed to identify the one they prefer—this indicates that there may be some uncertainty as to authorial intent even with these great Bible expositors. The best explanation of this aspect of Bible interpretation I have found is in Robert L. Plummer's excellent book *40 Questions About Interpreting the Bible* (Grand Rapids, MI: Kregel Publications, 2010). See especially Chapter 15, "Can A Text Have More Than One Meaning?" pages 135-142.

[140] There may be, however, many possible **applications**.

Additionally, on some points God is simply silent, as when He withholds the exact timing of Christ's Second Coming,[141] or how to completely reconcile the teachings in Scripture about the sovereignty of God and the free will and responsibility of man (both are taught in the Scripture, neither to the exclusion of the other), or who the author of the Book of Hebrews was. In such cases, we must admit that we just don't (yet) know for sure. We do know that all Scripture is **inspired** by God and is profitable for us to study (II Timothy 3:16-17):

> Inspiration…is the determining influence exercised by the Holy Spirit on the writers of the Old and New Testaments in order that they might proclaim and set down in an exact and authentic way the message as received from God. This influence guided them even to the extent of their use of words, that they might be kept from all error and omission.[142]

We also know that the Holy Spirit can enlighten **our** hearts and minds to understand a given text. (An important note here: This does not supplant the intellectual rigor involved in the interpretation process; it complements, facilitates and augments it.) This is a process referred to as *illumination*. **Illumination** occurs when we are **dwelling** in Christ. As René Pache explains,

> [Illumination is] the supernatural help granted by the Spirit of God to the reader of holy Scripture, to enable him to lay hold on the divine message…. Illumination is

---

[141] In Matthew 24:36 Jesus says, "But of that day and hour no one knows, not even the angels of heaven, nor the Son, but the Father alone."

[142] Pache, René. *The Inspiration and Authority of Scripture* (Chicago: Moody Press, 1969), p. 45.

normally permanent and increasing. From the time the believer submits to the Spirit of God, the Spirit leads him into all truth (John 16:13). For the converted heart, the Lord takes away the veil that obscures the reading...in proportion as we persevere in meditating on the word of God and in putting it into practice, our horizons widen and our comprehension of it increases.[143]

One of the great fallacies in interpretation is to assume that the Holy Spirit will reveal the correct meaning of a passage entirely apart from the application of intellectual rigor in our own minds. J.P. Moreland does an excellent job of refuting this idea in his book *Love Your God with All Your Mind: The Role of Reason in the Life of the Soul.*[144] He cites three proof texts that are commonly misinterpreted in support of this erroneous position: I Corinthians 2:14-15, John 4:26 and I John 2:27. From my personal experience, illumination most frequently occurs as the Holy Spirit brings to my mind other passages of Scripture that relate to the one I am focusing upon and trying to interpret.

A great example of why intellectual rigor is necessary in the process of interpretation is found in Ezekiel 37, the vision God gave to Ezekiel of a valley of dry bones being resuscitated and clothed with living flesh again. Many sermons have been preached applying this text to God's desire to bring revival in the Church. No question, God desires revival in the Church; **but** this particular vision applies to God's restoration of the nation of Israel during the coming Millennium to its original

---

[143] Ibid., p. 199.

[144] J.P. Moreland. *Love Your God with All Your Mind: The Role of Reason in the Life of the Soul* (Colorado Springs: Nav Press, 2012), pp. 47-51.

homeland. In fact, the vision is explicitly explained in the text itself, to be **observed** by the one studying it:

> Then He said to me, "Son of man, **these bones are the whole house of Israel**; behold, they say, 'Our bones are dried up and our hope has perished. We are completely cut off.' Therefore prophesy and say to them, 'Thus says the Lord God, "Behold, I will open your graves and cause you to come up out of your graves, My people; and **I will bring you into the land of Israel**. Then you will know that I am the Lord, when I have opened your graves and caused you to come up out of your graves, My people. I will put My Spirit within you and you will come to life, and I will place you on your own land. Then you will know that I, the Lord, have spoken and done it," declares the Lord.'"
> (Ezekiel 37:11-14) [emphasis added]

Interestingly, as it relates to our theme of dwelling, the text goes on to add,

> ...I will make a covenant of peace with them; it will be an everlasting covenant with them. And I will place them and multiply them, and will set My sanctuary in their midst forever. **My dwelling place also will be with them**; and I will be their God, and they will be My people. And the nations will know that I am the Lord who sanctifies Israel, when My sanctuary is in their midst forever. (Ezekiel 37:26-28) [emphasis added]

I would submit that the Holy Spirit would not somehow mysteriously illuminate this passage to mean anything contradicting its authorial intent, and that His illumination would rightfully involve intellectual rigor on the part of the interpreter to simply recognize what the text clearly explains.

4. **Application.** In making applications from a passage studied, consider whether there may be such things as an example to follow, a command to obey, a sin to forsake or a promise to claim. Some of the greatest applications I have found are simply to take comfort in certain truths about God (for example, His covenantal lovingkindness)—I suppose these could be referred to as *implications* (either for me or for others), rather than *applications*. As an example of what I am referring to here, consider John 11:35, "Jesus wept." The context of this verse is Jesus' arrival at the tomb of his friend Lazarus, who had died while Jesus deliberately delayed his coming. Jesus stated that this was necessary for the glory of God, more specifically to demonstrate that He, Himself, was the Resurrection and the Life. This was not a calloused pronouncement on the part of Jesus, as demonstrated by His weeping over His friend's death and over the grief of those who loved him, even knowing as He did the ultimate outcome, that He would raise Lazarus from the dead. One implication of this is that He was completely human, in addition to being completely God. A further implication of this truth is that he retains His humanity, even now in heaven, and is able to completely empathize with us in our sorrow, weakness and imperfect knowledge. The application of these great truths to my own life is that I can take great comfort in the compassion and relationship focus He has even now for me. I used my mind to arrive at these conclusions, and the Spirit illuminated these truths for me to apply them to my life.

Being visually oriented, I have attempted to summarize this entire process of Bible study as follows:

Application of intellectual rigor under the illumination* of the Holy Spirit as we observe, correlate and interpret	→	Authorial intent (in original language)	→	Application/ implication of this truth to life under the illumination* of the Holy Spirit

*Illumination occurs as one dwells in Christ.

Some great verses on use of our minds include:

When asked by a Pharisee to identify the greatest commandment in the Bible, Jesus replied,

"You shall love the Lord your God with all your heart, and with all your soul, and **with all your mind."** (Matthew 22:37)

Therefore I urge you, brethren, by the mercies of God, to present your bodies a living and holy sacrifice, acceptable to God, *which is* your spiritual service of worship. And do not be conformed to this world, but **be transformed by the renewing of your mind**, so that you may prove what the will of God is, that which is good and acceptable and perfect. (Romans 12:1-2)

And here are some great verses on illumination—again, from René Pache:[145]

I pray that **the eyes of your heart may be enlightened**, so that you will know what is the hope of His calling, what are

---

[145] These verses were taken from René Pache's *The Inspiration and Authority of Scripture*. (Chicago: Moody Press, 1969), page 208.

the riches of the glory of His inheritance in the saints (Ephesians 1:18), and that you be renewed in **the spirit of your mind...** (Ephesians 4:23)

For this reason also, since the day we heard *of it*, we have not ceased to pray for you and to ask **that you may be filled with the knowledge of His will in all spiritual wisdom and understanding,** so that you will walk in a manner worthy of the Lord, to please *Him* in all respects, bearing fruit in every good work and **increasing in the knowledge of God...** (Colossians 1:9-10)

Then He opened their minds to understand the Scriptures. (Luke 24:45)

A woman named Lydia, from the city of Thyatira, a seller of purple fabrics, a worshiper of God, was listening; and **the Lord opened her heart to respond to the things spoken by Paul.** (Acts 16:14)

In addition, the Bible frequently uses the metaphor of light and darkness to represent spiritual illumination or righteous living (as in John 1) and its opposite, spiritual darkness or blindness. God brings about the latter also, as in the case of Pharaoh (Exodus 7:13), Israel (Romans 11:25) and unsaved people (Ephesians 2:1-7). See also I Corinthians 2:14:

But a natural man does not accept the things of the Spirit of God, for they are foolishness to him; and he cannot understand them, because they are spiritually appraised.

For someone seeking to meditate on the Word and dwell in Christ, the importance of Scripture memory cannot be overstated. In Psalms 119:11, the psalmist says, "Your word I have **treasured** [or 'laid up' in the KJV] in my heart, / That I may not sin against You." God commanded Joshua, "This book of the law shall not depart from your mouth, but **you shall meditate on it day and night**, so that you may be careful to do according to all that is written in it; for then you will make your way prosperous, and then you will have success" (Joshua 1:8). Practically speaking, how then does one meditate? **Unfortunately, within the last several decades, the word *meditation* has come to mean something completely foreign to the Biblical concept.** What is currently said to be meditation is often actually pagan, Eastern, pantheistic monism. The term *mindfulness* is also often employed currently to denote a state of acute awareness of the present moment with a direction of the thoughts inward, effectively creating a mental and spiritual vacuum, to be filled with an awareness of one's connection to the earth and to other people.[146] The spiritual world, however, abhors such a vacuum:

> Now when the unclean spirit goes out of a man, it passes through waterless places seeking rest, and does not find *it*. Then it says, 'I will return to my house from which I came'; and when it comes, it finds *it* unoccupied, swept, and put in order. Then it goes and takes along with it seven other spirits more wicked than itself, and they go in and live there; and the last state of that man becomes worse than the first. That is the way it will also be with this evil generation. (Matthew 12:43-45)

Another current aberration from the Biblical concept of meditation is the practice known as *manifesting*. This is just

---

[146] Dr. Peter Jones has established an important ministry to address such issues, named TruthXchange. This ministry has published many excellent resources on the topic. <truthxchange.com>

essentially the old concept of positive thinking, but here it is "on steroids." It also has incorporated a spiritual element that convinces adherents they may actually wish into existence the object of their aspirations. Again, there is no reference here to a transcendent, sovereign, loving God who answers prayers; or if there is, it intends to manipulate this God into doing the will of the person who is meditating. Another common thread of thought along these same lines is to further imagine that we ourselves are actually God, and as God we are the center of our own individual universe! This same God is often said to be in each individual. You can see how this line of thought complements embracing the idol of self, as with self-actualization being the goal of each person's existence. This was discussed earlier in **Chapter 1.3** under "Hindrances to Dwelling." What a sharp contrast to the Christian concept of meditation!

The Christian interpretation of meditation is to be always, ultimately, focused upon the Word of God. A person who does so will be blessed, as described in Psalms 1:1-3:

> How blessed is the man who does not walk in the counsel of the wicked,
> Nor stand in the path of sinners,
> Nor sit in the seat of scoffers!
> But his delight is in the law of the Lord,
> And **in His law he meditates day and night**.
> He will be like a tree *firmly* planted by streams of water,
> Which yields its fruit in its season
> And its leaf does not wither;
> And in whatever he does, he prospers.

For me, the saddest verses in the Bible are Matthew 7:21-23. Jesus is speaking about the Great White Throne Judgment where he will address those who are to be condemned:[147]

> Not everyone who says to Me, 'Lord, Lord,' will enter the kingdom of heaven, but he who does the will of My Father who is in heaven *will enter.* Many will say to Me on that day, 'Lord, Lord, did we not prophesy in Your name, and in Your name cast out demons, and in Your name perform many miracles?' And then I will declare to them, '**I never knew you**; depart from Me, you who practice lawlessness.'

The question is, "How are we to know that we **know** God?" As I write this, I just learned that J.I. Packer passed away. His classic book *Knowing God* was published in 1973. In it, he distinguishes knowledge **of** God from knowledge **about** God. In so doing, he underscores the crucial role of meditation (with the best **definition of meditation** I have ever found):

> We must seek, in studying God, to be led to God. It was for this purpose that revelation was given, and it is to this use that we must put it…. How are we to do this? The rule for doing this is demanding, but simple. It is that we turn each truth we learn *about* God into matter for meditation *before* God, leading to prayer and praise *to* God…. Meditation is the activity of calling to mind, and thinking over, and dwelling on, and applying to oneself, the various things that one knows about the works and the ways and the purposes and promises of God. It is an activity of holy thought, consciously performed in the presence of God, under the eye of God, by the help of God, as a means of communion with God. Its

---

[147] Refer to **Appendix 4,** which gives an outline of events in the End Times.

purpose is to clear one's mental and spiritual vision of God, to let His truth make its full and proper impact on one's mind and heart. It is a matter of talking to oneself about God and oneself; it is, indeed, often a matter of arguing with oneself, reasoning oneself out of moods of doubt and unbelief into a clear apprehension of God's power and grace. Its effect is ever to humble us, as we contemplate God's greatness and glory, and our own littleness and sinfulness, and to encourage and reassure us—"comfort" us, in the old, strong Bible sense of the word—as we contemplate the unsearchable riches of divine mercy displayed in the Lord Jesus Christ.[148]

The more time one spends hearing, reading, studying and memorizing the Word, the more readily is the Holy Spirit able to call to mind certain passages as the need occurs in daily life. Meditation occurs as one ponders the application of these phrases or passages to daily life. Also, as one hears, reads, studies or memorizes, meditation occurs as the Scripture is turned over and re-examined from different angles in one's mind. This involves asking questions and noticing the features discussed earlier as a checklist for observation in Bible study. Meditation could be described as "mental chewing." Cows spend their mornings filling their stomachs with food, only to lie down in the shade in early afternoon to chew their "cud," which is the food ingested earlier. It is in chewing the cud that they gain the greatest flavor and satisfaction from what they have earlier eaten! So, in addition to meditating as we move through the day, we should devote regular time to pondering, re-reading, even praying aloud passages that the Holy Spirit impresses upon our hearts. This is where I most often land on the passages I have underlined or highlighted in my

---

148 Packer, J.I. _Knowing God._ Downers Grove, IL: InterVarsity Press, 1973. pp. 18-19.

Bible. In addition, I usually put my thoughts into my journal as I meditate. Someone once said, "**If you know how to worry, you know how to meditate!**"[149] That makes me realize that I can (with the help of the Holy Spirit) always redirect my mind from chewing on my problems to chewing on the Word. Also, instead of worrying over my problems, I can ask God to help me find a Biblical solution to them. So, from the above, it should be obvious how meditation on the Word is related to dwelling in Christ, if Christ **is** the Word made flesh (John 1). Time spent meditating on the Word is time spent dwelling with Him!

For Further Thought:

1. What is the "Holy Grail" of Bible study (refer to the notes for this chapter)?

2. What is the difference between inspiration and illumination?

3. Which comes first, interpretation or application, and why is that important?

4. What does it mean to meditate?

5. How is Biblical meditation different from what is being referred to today in our culture as meditation?

6. How are studying and meditating on the Word related to dwelling?

7. What is my personal plan for hearing, reading, studying, memorizing and meditating on the Word of God?

8. What is Satan's objective for us as regards the Word of God?

---

[149] I was unable to identify the original source; although, the Internet attributes it to more than one person.

Chapter 7

Sit, Walk and Stand – Dwelling While "On the Road"

Therefore be careful how you walk, not as unwise men but as wise, making the most of your time, because the days are evil. (Ephesians 5:15-16)

It has been observed by others that the Bible employs several different bodily postures as figures representing different aspects of the Christian life. At least four of these are found in the Book of Ephesians alone: sitting (1:17-21, 2:6-9), kneeling (3:14), walking (4:1), and standing (6:10-11, 13-18).[150] Let us follow Watchman Nee's classic little book *Sit, Walk, Stand: The Process of Christian Maturity*[151] in considering three of these as they relate to the

---

[150] Omitted here is *running* (I Corinthians 9:24-27, Hebrews 12:1, Psalms 119:32, Isaiah 40:31).

[151] Nee, Watchman. *Sit, Walk, Stand: The Process of Christian Maturity* (Fort Washington, PA: CLC Publications, 2009). This is a compilation from Mr. Watchman Nee's spoken ministry. He died in 1972, having established over 200

concept of dwelling in Christ. For Nee, the process of Christian maturity begins with sitting:

> God has made us to **sit** with Christ in the heavenly places, and every Christian must begin his spiritual life from that place of rest (Ephesians 2:6).... In walking or standing we expend a great deal of energy, but when we are **seated** we relax at once because the strain no longer falls on our muscles and nerves but upon something outside of ourselves. So also in the spiritual realm, to **sit** down is simply to rest our whole weight—our load, ourselves, our future, everything—upon the Lord.... Our keyword here is not, of course, in its context, a command to "sit down," but to see ourselves as **seated** in Christ. (Nee 9, 13, 14)

In other words, we must **rest** in the finished work of Christ and rely completely upon His provision. Here is the connection to dwelling. It is only through our union with Him (the phrase "in Him" or "in Christ" is repeated no less than 35 times in the Book of Ephesians) that we will ever accomplish anything of spiritual value, anything that will stand the test of fire at the Judgment Seat of Christ.[152]

In the Book of Ephesians, chapters 1 through 3 are about what it means to be seated with Christ in the heavenlies. These chapters are primarily theological in nature. The last three chapters are by contrast practical in nature—they outline how a Christian should walk if indeed the theology of the first three chapters is true.

---

churches in China, and he was imprisoned his last twenty years on false charges.

[152] The Judgment Seat of Christ, or *Bema* (II Corinthians 5:9-11), is the believer's judgment of works, not the Great White Throne, a judgment of unbelievers. Refer to **Appendix 4** for a graphical explanation.

Ephesians 4:1 begins with the word *therefore*. The whole book hinges on this word. It refers to all that has been said in the first three chapters about being seated with Christ:

> **Therefore** I, the prisoner of the Lord, implore you to **walk** in a manner worthy of the calling with which you have been called...

The early disciples certainly continued dwelling with Christ as they followed Him. So should we. Nee is emphatic that when we begin to walk, we do not cease sitting, dwelling and resting:

> **Sitting describes our position with Christ in the heavenlies. Walking is the practical outworking of that position here on earth.**... Eight times in Ephesians the word walk is used. It means literally "to walk around," and is used here figuratively by Paul to mean "to comport oneself, to order one's behavior".... Forsake for a moment our place of rest in Him, and immediately we are tripped, and our testimony in the world is marred. But abide [we might use the word *dwell* here] in Christ, and our position there ensures the power to walk worthy of Him here.... Paul has seen himself seated in Christ; therefore his walk before men takes its character from Christ **dwelling** in him. Small wonder that he prays for the Ephesians "that Christ may **dwell** in your hearts through faith" (Ephesians 3:17).[153]

But the word *walk* carries a further meaning: "It suggests first conduct or behavior, but it also contains in it the idea of progress toward a goal:"[154]

---

[153] Nee, pp. 23, 24, 29, 30.
[154] Ibid., p. 36.

Therefore be careful how you **walk**, not as unwise men but as wise, making the most of [or redeeming] your time, because the days are evil. So then do not be foolish, but understand what the will of the Lord is. (Ephesians 5:15-17) [emphasis added]

I press on toward the goal for the prize of the upward call of God in Christ Jesus. (Philippians 3:14)

One word of caution here: We may always know in general terms where we are headed, because our hope is fixed in heaven at the revealing of Christ. It is not, however, always possible for us to see God's exact strategy in every detail about how we will get there. I think about Abraham (or Abram as he was known then) being called from Ur of the Chaldeans (Babylon) to set out on a several-hundred-mile journey to the Promised Land. As far as I can tell, the Scriptures are silent about how much God revealed to Abraham about the destination of his journey on a day-by-day basis.

By faith Abraham, when he was called, obeyed by going out to a place which he was to receive for an inheritance; and **he went out, not knowing where he was going**. By faith he lived as an alien in the land of promise, as in a foreign *land*, dwelling in tents with Isaac and Jacob, fellow heirs of the same promise; for he was looking for the city which has foundations, whose architect and builder is God. (Hebrews 11:8-10) [emphasis added]

I think the point here is that Abraham had one day's guidance at a time, much as the Hebrews in the desert wanderings had with the pillars of fire and smoke. This in my mind also relates to the fact that God reveals his will to us (our "marching orders" in the

Church Age) much as He provides for our needs—that is, in "day-tight increments," he instructs us to "let the day's own trouble be sufficient for the day." Again Matthew 6:33-34 speaks to us here. It is wise to make long-range plans (as the book of Proverbs instructs us to), when they are committed to God (indeed, "Abraham was going to a place he was to receive for an inheritance...a city which has foundations whose architect and builder is God," much as we are), but we must never allow our plans to take our eyes off the Savior as he leads us day-by-day (Hebrews 12:1-3). We must be prepared for God-directed interruptions or redirections of our plans.

Come now, you who say, "Today or tomorrow we will go to such and such a city, and spend a year there and engage in business and make a profit." Yet you do not know what your life will be like tomorrow. You are *just* a vapor that appears for a little while and then vanishes away. (James 4:13-14)

In fact, there are well over fifty verses in the Bible addressing this concept of walking in a manner worthy of pleasing God. To name just a few: It is possible to walk in light or to walk in darkness (I John 1:7). We are to walk in the Spirit (Galatians 5:25). We are to walk by faith and not by sight (II Corinthians 5:7). He will direct our path when we acknowledge Him in all our ways (Proverbs 3:5-6).

In a word: We must walk (and here's that key word again) with **integrity**. Psalms 15:1-2 connects walking to our earlier discussions of integrity and dwelling:

O Lord, who may **abide** in Your tent?
Who may **dwell** on Your holy hill?

He who **walks** with **integrity**, and works righteousness,
And speaks truth in his heart. (Psalms 15:1-2)

The last twenty-five verses of Ephesians 6 conclude the practical portion of the book, with a discussion of a final bodily posture, **standing**. This is the famous description of the armor that the Christian must put on to **stand** against the wiles of our enemy, Satan.

> Finally, **be strong** in the Lord and in the strength of His might. Put on the full armor of God, so that you will be able to **stand firm** against the schemes of the devil. For our struggle is not against flesh and blood, but against the rulers, against the powers, against the world forces of this darkness, against the spiritual forces of wickedness in the heavenly places. Therefore, take up the full armor of God, so that you will be able to **resist** in the evil day, and having done everything, to **stand firm**. **Stand firm** therefore, having girded your loins with truth, and having put on the breastplate of righteousness, and having shod your feet with the preparation of the gospel of peace; in addition to all, taking up the shield of faith with which you will be able to extinguish all the flaming arrows of the evil one. And take the helmet of salvation, and the sword of the Spirit, which is the word of God. (Ephesians 6:10-17)

Nee draws an interesting distinction here:

> The word "stand" implies that the ground disputed by the Enemy is really God's, and therefore ours. We need not struggle to gain a foothold on it. **Nearly all the weapons of our warfare in Ephesians are purely defensive**.... And that is precisely the difference between the warfare waged by the

Lord Jesus and the warfare waged by us. His was offensive; our is, in essence, defensive.... Our task is one of holding, not of attacking.... Thus, today we do not fight *for* victory. We fight *from* victory.[155] [emphasis added]

In other words, we always fight from a **position** (seated in the heavenlies in Christ) in which we are "more than conquerors" (Romans 8:37). The key to victory in any spiritual conflict is, therefore, to remember who we are and whose we are, to continue **dwelling** in Christ under his shield:[156]

> Therefore, prepare your minds for action, keep sober in spirit, fix your hope completely on the grace to be brought to you at the revelation of Jesus Christ. (1 Peter 1:13)

To summarize, we are to **walk** with integrity as those who are dwelling in Christ, "fixing our eyes" on Him (Hebrews 12:1-2), even as we remain seated in the heavenlies.

---

[155] Ibid., pp. 47, 48. The point here is that we are always to follow behind our Lord in spiritual battle; we are never to precede Him. As Henry Blackaby points out in his book *Experiencing God*, our job is to see where the LORD is already working and then to join Him there (John 5:17), not to pick out a project on our own and then ask the LORD to follow us and bless it. In that sense, the LORD has already laid His claim and proclaimed victory over any battlefield we are called to. We are therefore defending what is already His. He, on the other hand, is the "breaker" (Micah 2:13) into new territory. Our enemy has already (ultimately) been defeated and condemned (his defeat has been decreed but not yet fully enacted). He just wants to drag as many of us as he can with him and rob the rest of us of our reward.

[156] An excellent resource on spiritual warfare is Chip Ingram's book *The Invisible War: What Every Believer Needs to Know About Satan, Demons and Spiritual Warfare* (Grand Rapids, MI: Baker Books, 2006).

For Further Thought:

1. What does it mean to walk with God? Is it possible to walk with God and dwell with Him at the same time? How is it possible to remain "seated in the heavenlies" even as we walk? In practical terms, what does it mean to walk with God?

2. What is the main prerequisite for walking with God?

3. What are the challenges in walking with God, and how might we overcome these? (Refer to the table at the end of **Chapter 9** entitled "Habits and Hindrances.")

4. Is the purpose of the armor of God primarily offensive or defensive? What does each piece represent in the life of the believer? In spiritual warfare, are we to lead or follow? Should we always have on the armor of God as we walk?

5. Must we always know God's detailed, explicit plan for our lives? In the absence of this, how are we to live? How is the concept of living in "day-tight increments" related to this? Is it wise to have a long-range plan? How should we respond when that plan is interrupted?

Chapter 8

Three Who Struggled and Prevailed in Dwelling

To get a better picture of how this all works out in daily life, let us briefly examine the lives of three believers who struggled but prevailed in dwelling: The Old Testament prophet Elijah, the New Testament apostle Paul, and the second king of Israel, David. In doing so, we will note how each abided, waited, prayed, rested, embraced the Scriptures and walked in obedience to the LORD, while possessing integrity.

The Prophet Elijah

Nothing is known of the prophet Elijah prior to his appearance in the Biblical narrative in I Kings 17. He was a prophet to the Northern Kingdom in the ninth century BC, during the reign of King Ahab (a wicked king, as were most kings in the Northern Kingdom). He is perhaps most famous for his encounter with the 450 prophets of Baal atop Mount Carmel in I Kings 18, and his subsequent flight into the wilderness to escape the avenging wrath of wicked Queen Jezebel. Jezebel had led the nation into idolatry in worshiping the pagan god Baal, and Elijah had foretold an extended drought in consequence (I Kings 17:1). Elijah first challenges the pagan priests, then mocks their unsuccessful attempts to call down fire on a sacrifice that Elijah had directed be set up there. Verse 18 in Chapter 21 is significant, for it reveals Elijah's **integrity**. He challenges the people of Israel before himself calling down the fire: "How long *will* you hesitate between two opinions? If the Lord is God, follow Him; but if Baal, follow him." But the people did not say a word in response, thus displaying their **double-mindedness**. They were seeking to combine worship of the true God with Baal worship. Elijah then succeeds in spectacular fashion where the pagan priests had failed in calling down fire to consume the sacrifice. Following that, he personally slays all 450 priests (I Kings 18:40) before fleeing into the wilderness because of Jezebel's threatened retribution. There, in the midst of his fear and depression, he requests of the LORD that he might just die. An angel of the LORD then meets him there with food, and he travels in the strength of that food for forty days. It is significant that he ends up at Mount Horeb (Sinai), which is where God gave Moses the law. He wanted to be as close to his God as he could possibly get:

> Then he came there to a cave and lodged there; and behold, the word of the Lord *came* to him, and He said to him, "What are you doing here, Elijah?" He said, "I have been very zealous for the Lord, the God of hosts; for the sons of Israel have forsaken Your covenant, torn down Your altars and killed Your prophets with the sword. And I alone am left; and they seek my life, to take it away." (I Kings 19:9-10)

In the wilderness Elijah hides, waiting in the cave in utter fear (of Jezebel's threat to take his life and with the mistaken notion that he is the only true follower of God left in Israel), exhaustion, despair and discouragement, even asking the LORD to take his life, until the LORD speaks again to Him. After first using a strong wind, an earthquake and a fire, in "a sound of a gentle blowing" (I Kings 19:12), the LORD instructs him to arise and return to civilization (Damascus) and there anoint the next king of Israel and Elisha, as his mentee, and eventually the next prophet in his place. The gentle blowing brings to my mind Psalms 46:10-11:

"Cease *striving* ["Be still" in the KJV] and know that I am God;
I will be exalted among the nations, I will be exalted in the earth."

The Lord of hosts is with us;
The God of Jacob is our stronghold. *Selah.*

Here we can see Elijah **resting** before the LORD before resuming his **walk**, his next great movement in obedience to Him. Frequently, we find ourselves needing to withdraw from the chaos of the world around us to a quiet place, there to seek God and to refocus. We have the advantage over Elijah here in that we don't need to travel great distances to **dwell** with Him, when He **indwells** us. We need to frequently remind ourselves that the LORD is in control, and as long as we continue obeying Him **one day at a time**, He will shape the outcome—it will not come through our own striving. "The Lord of Hosts is with us; the God of Jacob is our stronghold." Amen. There seems to be a thread woven through the Scriptures communicating this idea of fleeing into the wilderness to find refuge in God. As we shall see, Paul found respite in the wilderness following his conversion on the Damascus Road. David expresses this idea beautifully in Psalms 55, which is directly addressed to God as a prayer:

My heart is in anguish within me,
And the terrors of death have fallen upon me.
Fear and trembling come upon me,
And horror has overwhelmed me.
I said, "Oh, that I had wings like a dove!
I would fly away and be at rest.
"Behold, I would wander far away,
I would lodge in the wilderness. *Selah.*
"I would hasten to my place of refuge
From the stormy wind *and* tempest." (Psalms 55:4-8)

The applications we might find in this for our own lives are (1) To ask ourselves how our feelings may be clouding our perception of reality, and (2) To consider occasionally escaping to a peaceful, quiet place, free from the distractions of the world, especially when we need to hear a fresh word from the LORD and to seek His face, gaining His perspective on the reality in our lives. In fact, we need not leave our homes to accomplish this. During one such time in our own lives, Sara and I went for a personal retreat to the Billy Graham Conference Center ("The Cove") in the beautiful North Carolina mountains. It turned out to be a pivotal experience for us both.

In all, Elijah performs at least nine miracles, mostly in response to his personal **prayers**—including resurrecting a dead person—and all this before being taken alive up into heaven on a flaming chariot (II Kings 2):

Elijah was a man with a nature like ours, and he **prayed** earnestly that it would not rain, and it did not rain on the earth for three years and six months. Then he **prayed** again, and the sky poured rain and the earth produced its fruit. (James 5:17-18)

The fact that he was highly regarded by the "School of, or Sons of [here meaning disciples of] the Prophets" (II Kings 2:3) indicates that he was knowledgeable about God's Word. At that time, God's written Word consisted of the Law, the Prophets and the Writings (Psalms, Job, Ecclesiastes and Song of Solomon). Many prophets of the true God had been killed in an earlier pogrom by Jezebel (I Kings 18:4). So Elijah was a **student of God's Word** at great personal risk. We are again at an advantage here, in having God's written Word so readily available for us to **abide** in.

Other noteworthy mentions of Elijah in the Bible include the following:

- Jesus mentions him in connection with John the Baptist in Matthew 11:13-15:

  For all the prophets and the Law prophesied until John. And if you are willing to accept *it*, John himself is Elijah who was to come. He who has ears to hear, let him hear.

- Jesus alludes in the above passage to a prophecy found in Malachi:

  Behold, I am going to send you Elijah the prophet before the coming of the great and terrible day of the Lord. He will restore the hearts of the fathers to *their* children and the hearts of the children to their fathers, so that I will not come and smite the land with a curse. (Malachi 4:5-6)

- John did in fact call the nation to repentance, but John himself, when asked if he were Elijah, denied it:

They asked him, "What then? Are you Elijah?" And he said, "I am not." "Are you the Prophet?" And he answered, "No." (John 1:21)

- Finally, on the Mount of Transfiguration, before his crucifixion, Jesus appears briefly in His glorified body, in conversation with Elijah and Moses, presumably discussing the events then about to take place:

And He was transfigured before them; and His face shone like the sun, and His garments became as white as light. And behold, Moses and Elijah appeared to them, talking with Him. (Matthew 17:2-3)

How, then, does Elijah dwell? For all of his momentous accomplishments, in Elijah we see a man who is completely human and vulnerable to periods of depression and fatigue. His refuge and strength in such times truly are always in the LORD. **Waiting** on the LORD, drawing strength from Him, **abiding** in Him, he is able to perform mighty miracles through his **prayers** and also amazing feats of physical endurance. We see him **resting** in the LORD, listening for His voice while in the wilderness cave. He evidently earns special favor from the LORD for his devotion in **dwelling**, as evidenced by his miraculous transport to heaven at the conclusion of his life, his appearance on the Mount of Transfiguration and his foretold appearance in the End Times. The way I am able to synthesize these prophecies is to assume they have a dual fulfillment, first in John the Baptist and again in the End Times, perhaps as one of the two mysterious witnesses mentioned in Revelation 11 (whose physical appearance and ability to call fire from heaven suggest the possibility). Beyond that, I must decline to speculate where the Scriptures are silent.

The Apostle Paul

The apostle Paul, that great persecutor of the early church, also went into the wilderness following his conversion on the Damascus Road:

> But when God, who had set me apart *even* from my mother's womb and called me through His grace, was pleased to reveal His Son in me so that I might preach Him among the Gentiles, I did not immediately consult with flesh and blood, nor did I go up to Jerusalem to those who were apostles before me; but I went away to Arabia, and returned once more to Damascus. Then three years later I went up to Jerusalem to become acquainted with Cephas, and stayed with him fifteen days. (Galatians 1:15-18)

Much ink has been devoted to debating whether Paul went to Mount Sinai, as did Elijah, during his journey into the Arabian wilderness to "regroup" before beginning his new mission for Christ, commencing in Damascus, and whether the three years were spent in Arabia or in Damascus (modern-day Syria). (Note that the Sinai Peninsula is not part of what we now refer to as the "Arabian Peninsula" [comprising modern-day Saudi Arabia, Kuwait, Qatar, Yemen and other nations], because the geopolitical boundaries at that time were much different.) The parallels are at least noteworthy. His motives for this sabbatical could have been to (1) establish his apostleship as stemming directly from Christ's appointment, with Whom he presumably communed while there, and not from men nor by his own making, (2) commune with Christ, **abiding** in Him, as **he poured over the law he had studied under Gamaliel** to understand how it and the prophecies all applied to his newly found faith, and (3) prepare himself emotionally for the demanding trials he knew he was about to endure, as per the expressed intentions of Christ,

Himself: "For I will show him how much he must endure for my name's sake" (Acts 9:16). The bottom line is that it has to have been a time of (1) **dwelling** with Christ ("not consulting with flesh and blood") and reflection (**meditation**) upon the **Scriptures** and (2) preparation of his soul for the challenges he knew he was about to face. It is unknown (but doubtful) whether Paul carried written copies of the Scriptures with him into the wilderness, but one has merely to examine his epistles, such as his letter to the Romans, to realize how thoroughly he had **studied** and memorized them.

It is also interesting to correlate the wilderness retreats of Paul and Elijah with those of Jesus (His temptation for forty days) and John the Baptist (raised in the wilderness), prior to their own assumptions of public ministry. The pattern seems to be that God calls us to retreat and **dwell** before He sends us to tell. The duration of Paul's time in Arabia is also debated. Although I find no support for the idea in the Acts 9 chronology, the mention of three years in Galatians 1:18 (above) leads me to believe that was the amount of time he spent either there or in Damascus or in the wilderness of Arabia (a lot depending upon whether Damascus was counted as part of Arabia at that time or not). Either way, those three years was quite a bit of time to prepare himself for what lay ahead for him after he returned to Jerusalem. He would go on to make three missionary journeys. Following that, he would be arrested in Jerusalem and, after many delays lasting years, be taken to Rome for trial and eventual execution (according to tradition). Again, Jesus had said about him, "I will show him much he must suffer for My name" (Acts 9:16). Paul recounts his experiences in fulfillment of this in his second letter to the Corinthians:

> But in whatever respect anyone *else* is bold—I speak in foolishness—I am just as bold myself. Are they Hebrews? So am I. Are they Israelites? So am I. Are they descendants of

Abraham? So am I. Are they servants of Christ?—I speak as if insane—I more so; in far more labors, in far more imprisonments, beaten times without number, often in danger of death. Five times I received from the Jews thirty-nine *lashes*. Three times I was beaten with rods, once I was stoned, three times I was shipwrecked, a night and a day I have spent in the deep. *I have been* on frequent journeys, in dangers from rivers, dangers from robbers, dangers from *my* countrymen, dangers from the Gentiles, dangers in the city, **dangers in the wilderness**, dangers on the sea, dangers among false brethren; *I have been* in labor and hardship, through many sleepless nights, in hunger and thirst, often without food, in cold and exposure. Apart from *such* external things, there is the daily pressure on me *of* concern for all the churches. Who is weak without my being weak? Who is led into sin without my intense concern? (II Corinthians 11:21-29)

Paul's **integrity**, his single focus following his conversion, his "**one thing**" was always "to press on" (Philippians 3:7-15):

[Speaking before hostile Jewish leaders] "I am a Jew, born in Tarsus of Cilicia, but brought up in this city, educated under Gamaliel, strictly according to the Law of our fathers, being zealous for God just as you all are today." (Acts 22:3)

But whatever things were gain to me, these things I have counted as loss because of Christ. More than that, I count all things to be loss in view of the surpassing value of knowing Christ Jesus my Lord, for whom I have suffered the loss of all things, and count them *mere* rubbish, so **that I may gain Christ**, and may be found in Him, not having a righteousness of my own derived from *the* Law, but that which is through faith in Christ, the righteousness which *comes* from God on the basis of faith, **that I may know Him** and the power of His resurrection and the fellowship of His sufferings, being conformed to His death; if somehow I may attain to the resurrection from the dead. Not that I have already grasped *it all* or have already become perfect, but I press on if I may also take hold of that for which I was even taken hold of by Christ Jesus. Brothers *and sisters*, I do not regard myself as having taken hold of *it yet*; but **one thing *I do***: forgetting what *lies* behind and reaching forward to what *lies* ahead, **I press on** toward the goal for the prize of the upward call of God in Christ Jesus. Therefore, all who are mature, let's have this attitude; and if in anything you have a different attitude, God will reveal that to you as well. (Philippians 3:7-15)

His contentment in circumstances—his **rest**—are also in evidence from such passages as the following:

Not that I speak from need, for I have learned to be content in whatever *circumstances* I am. I know how to get along with little, and I also know how to live in prosperity; in any and every *circumstance* I have learned the secret of being filled and going hungry, both of having abundance and suffering need. I can do all things through Him who strengthens me. (Philippians 4:11-13)

While **waiting** for his trial in Rome, he was delayed and put off by the Roman leaders for as long as two years in one place. He was able to rejoice in these setbacks because they gave him an even greater opportunity to advance the Gospel, as he **abided** in Christ. Paul's epistles, such as his letter to the Ephesians, contain many lengthy and eloquent **prayers and expressions of worship**, and his epistles also contain many instructions regarding how to **walk** as a Christian (refer to **Chapter 7** for more on **walking**).

However, lest we conclude that Paul was a perfect Christian following his conversion, he reveals to us his own struggles with sin in a poignant passage in Romans 7:15-25:

> For what I am doing, I do not understand; for I am not practicing what I *would* like to *do*, but I am doing the very thing I hate. But if I do the very thing I do not want *to do*, I agree with the Law, *confessing* that the Law is good. So now, no longer am I the one doing it, but sin which dwells in me. For I know that nothing good dwells in me, that is, in my flesh; for the willing is present in me, but the doing of the good *is* not. For the good that I want, I do not do, but I practice the very evil that I do not want. But if I am doing the very thing I do not want, I am no longer the one doing it, but sin which dwells in me. I find then the principle that evil is present in me, the one who wants to do good. For I joyfully concur with the law of God in the inner man, but I see a different law in the members of my body, waging war against the law of my mind and making me a prisoner of the law of sin which is in my members. Wretched man that I am! Who will set me free from the body of this death? Thanks be to God through Jesus Christ our Lord! So then, on the one hand I myself with my mind am serving the law of God, but on the other, with my flesh the law of sin.

What is significant to me in the above passage is that, despite the war we see raging within him, Paul is experiencing victory through what he is doing with his mind. That would be a great example for us to follow, and it would involve **our use of God's Word** in our own struggles. It should also give us great encouragement. Having prevailed, Paul was able to say at the conclusion of his life,

> I have fought the good fight, I have finished the course, I have kept the faith; in the future there is laid up for me the crown of righteousness, which the Lord, the righteous Judge, will award to me on that day; and not only to me, but also to all who have loved His appearing. (II Timothy 4:7-8)

Old Testament King David

We most often hear of David in the context of his great accomplishments, as in his victory over Goliath; and of God's favor on him, commencing even before Samuel anointed hm as a young boy. Acts 13:22 tells us that God famously said of David, "I have found in David the son of Jesse, a man after my own heart, who will do all my will." God later says that He intends to establish David's throne throughout eternity. But the fact remains that David also struggled and failed in grand fashion in at least two important respects: His sin with Bathsheba, and Uriah her husband, and his parenting failures, resulting ultimately in a tragically dysfunctional family and the death of 20,000 Israelites, including his rebellious son Absalom. So, can it be said that David dwelt with God? I believe the answer to this question is "yes; but in doing so, he also struggled and failed (as we all do), suffered the consequences, and ultimately prevailed." David's many wives were the major source of his problems, even as his earlier lust for Bathsheba had led him to commit adultery and then murder to cover it up:

> Now, David already had several wives when he began his reign, but after he became king he took even more (2 Samuel 5:13). It was David's accumulation of wives, in express violation of Deuteronomy 17:17, that contributed to much

familial strife and a great deal of pain to the people of Israel. But the issue wasn't with the wives themselves, or even that these wives drew David away to idolatry like Solomon, it was the secondary effects of polygamy that stirred up strife in the house of David. You see, these many wives produced many children for David—sisters, brothers, half-sisters, and half-brothers—and this is where the problems began.[157]

David's love for his children caused him to turn a blind eye to their wrongdoing. Parental love becomes idolatry.

In 2 Samuel 13:1-22, we encounter three of David's children, Absalom and Tamar who were full siblings (they had the same mother) and Amnon who was their half-brother. Amnon is seized by a perverse desire for his half-sister Tamar and pretends to be sick so she will take care of him. But when she comes to tend to his illness, he violates her. When this horrible thing happened to David's own daughter, by one of his own sons, you would expect the king of Israel to respond with a demand for justice. And that's what Absalom expected too—this was his full-sister after all. But instead, all he got from David was actionless anger (2 Samuel 13:21-22). Amnon was left unpunished. This is where we begin to see Absalom's root of bitterness first begin to bud.[158]

Absalom takes justice into his own hands by murdering Amnon in revenge, again without a response from David. Absalom's anger blossoms into hatred for his father and a conviction that David is unfit to govern. He organizes a military force that causes David to

---

[157] Reagan Rose, "When Leaders Fail to Discipline Their Children," *The Master's Seminary Blog*, 14 August 2018. Accessed 21 December 2020. <blog.tms.edu/leaders-fail-discipline-children>
[158] Ibid.

flee Jerusalem. II Samuel 16:21-22 tells us that, acting on bad counsel, Absalom then pitches a tent on the roof of the palace, where he sleeps with his father's concubines/wives. While running from Absalom and his army, David finally finds time to **dwell** with his LORD, and in doing so writes Psalms 3, which is a **prayer** addressed directly to the LORD:

> O Lord, how my adversaries have increased!
> Many are rising up against me.
> ² Many are saying of my soul,
> "There is no deliverance for him in God." *Selah.*
>
> ³ **But You, O Lord, are a shield about me,**
> **My glory, and the One who lifts my head.**
> ⁴ **I was crying to the Lord with my voice,**
> **And He answered me from His holy mountain.** *Selah.*
> ⁵ **I lay down and slept;**
> **I awoke, for the Lord sustains me.**
> ⁶ I will not be afraid of ten thousands of people
> Who have set themselves against me round about.
>
> ⁷ Arise, O Lord; save me, O my God!
> For You have smitten all my enemies on the cheek;
> You have shattered the teeth of the wicked.
> ⁸ Salvation belongs to the Lord;
> Your blessing *be* upon Your people! *Selah.*

Here we see David's heart in the way that God saw it—despite his colossal mistakes, David keeps returning to His one true refuge and strength to **dwell** in safety. In verse 5 we see him **resting** in complete reliance upon the LORD's protection. Verse 3 is one of my all-time favorites—"lifting my head" could be rescue from shame, despair and discouragement. Psalm 4, also written by David, continues with this same theme in verse 8:

> In peace I will both lie down and sleep,
> For You alone, O Lord, make me to **dwell** in safety.

Absalom is eventually killed following a battle in which 20,000 hapless victims perish. The LORD directly intervenes by causing Absalom's hair to be entangled in the branches of a tree he rides beneath, whereupon David's soldiers fall upon him.

Following his sin with Bathsheba, when Nathan the prophet comes to confront David, Nathan says the following to him: "the sword will not depart from the house of David" (2 Samuel 12:10). So, despite David's moving confession in Psalms 51 and 32 in response, there were consequences for David's sin, as we have seen them unfold in the above events.

What is it, then, about David that draws God's favor upon Him, despite his failures? It could not be that he led a sinless life. It has to have been that David's true home, his *oikos*,[159] his settling-down place, his dwelling place, the place he also came running back to when life got beyond him, was the LORD, Himself. And there he **rested** and **prayed** and **worshipped** and sang praises (and wrote Psalms!). The LORD would not allow David to build the temple because of the blood he had shed and the mistakes he had made, but David raised the money to finance the temple so that his son Solomon could build it. As he was handing off power to Solomon just before his death, in his prayer David makes reference to God's interest in **integrity**, and His

---

[159] Refer to the word study on *dwell* in **Appendix 1**.

focus upon David's heart and the hearts of His people. David's prayer included the following:

> **Since I know, O my God, that You try the heart** and delight in uprightness, I, **in the integrity of my heart**, have willingly offered all these *things*; so now with joy I have seen Your people, who are present here, make *their* offerings willingly to You. O Lord, the God of Abraham, Isaac and Israel, our fathers, **preserve this forever in the intentions of the heart of Your people, and direct their heart to You; and give to my son Solomon a perfect heart** to keep Your commandments, Your testimonies and Your statutes, and to do *them* all, and to build the temple, for which I have made provision." (I Chronicles 29:17-19)

Was he a perfect king? Not by any means—much as we saw with Paul, David struggles with sin. Was he "a man after God's own heart" who ultimately prevailed? Yes, absolutely, and this should give great hope and encouragement to us all!

For Further Thought:

1. How did each man dwell, abide, wait, pray, worship, rest, study, meditate, walk and possess integrity?

2. One common thread in these men is their great passion and strength of resolve in the midst of tremendous trials. They were not lukewarm, as was the church in Laodicea (in Revelation 2). What are some other common threads? What can we learn from this?

3. With which of these three men can you most readily identify and why?

4. What most challenges you from the lives of these men?

5. What most comforts and encourages you?

6. What do these three men each have in common with the list of heroes of the faith found in Hebrews 11? Are any of them perfect? What comfort and encouragement can you derive from that?

Part III

Summary and Conclusion

Chapter 9

He Who Dwells

We have seen how "he who dwells" is one who has given himself or herself to be Christ's home and is actively seeking refuge and shelter in Christ, and in so doing has become one who also **abides, rests, waits,** (watches), **prays,** (fasts), **worships, studies, meditates,** (sits), **walks** (and stands), all in Christ. As mentioned earlier, the eight actions in boldface seem to be the core commands. As we have seen, the LORD directs us to do these things. We should not, however, think of these commands as a list of burdensome edicts that we must somehow juggle and follow using our own resources. We are simply to "Love the lord our God with all of our heart, soul, mind and strength, and love our neighbor as our self" (Matthew 22:37). When we do this, the Holy Spirit will lead and empower us, and even give us the desire to accomplish these other activities as well. Philippians 2:13 states "…for it is God who is at work in you, both to will and to work for *His* good pleasure." Many followers of Christ do these activities without even consciously identifying them by name. They just know they are drawn to do them. Still, I hope you have found it helpful to define and explore the meaning of each of these. We should be able to recognize these habits forming in our lives as we go about following Christ.

The questions I have been learning to ask myself as I have been putting these ideas together are, "Am I dwelling in Christ right now? If not, why? What is lacking?" I know that Christ is dwelling in me, but am I actively seeking to dwell in Him? I find the activity I must constantly seek to improve is prayer, particularly the focused, intentional type of intercessory prayer; and also praise, specifically that type of praise that employs the Psalms to be read out loud. Of the five hindrances to dwelling listed in **Chapter 1.3**—idolatry, Biblical illiteracy or apathy, busyness, negativity and legalism—the "nattering nabobs of negativism"[160] seem to be what I am most often challenged by. Through my personal experience with chronic back pain and depression (my "thorns in the flesh") mentioned earlier, the LORD has given me an opportunity to learn to rely upon Him as my joy and strength as I "work out [my] salvation in fear and trembling" (Philippians 2:2). It will be a work-in-progress until the Resurrection. Paul, speaking of his unidentified thorn in the flesh, famously said (after asking God to remove his thorn three times):

> And He has said to me, "My grace is sufficient for you, for [my] power is perfected in weakness." Most gladly, therefore, I will rather boast about my weaknesses, so that the power of Christ may **dwell** in me. (II Corinthians 12:9)

In Romans 7:15-25, Paul also describes a battle raging between his "inner man," in which he "joyfully concurs with the law of God" (verse 22), and his flesh, "in which nothing good **dwells**" (verse 18). My task is to make sure my flesh is not feeding my impulse

---

[160] From a speech written by William Safire for Vice President Spiro Agnew in 1970.

toward negativity.[161] Instead, I shall seek, by the Spirit's enabling, to redirect my thoughts according to Philippians 4:8:

> Finally, brethren, whatever is true, whatever is honorable, whatever is right, whatever is pure, whatever is lovely, whatever is of good repute, if there is any excellence and if anything worthy of praise, **dwell** on these things.

The word *dwell* here is, as mentioned earlier, an intransitive verb, which means an action we take upon ourselves, but in this instance, it is also an imperative mood verb, which means that it is a command, not a suggestion. That's **my** own challenge. It can be a tough thicket to fight through, but that's how I am seeking to overcome negativity and to **dwell** in Christ in the process, relying on the Holy Spirit's power. As we saw earlier in **Chapter 2** on "Our Part in Dwelling," and also in **Chapter 5** on "Rest," D. Martyn Lloyd-Jones has captured this idea when he says, "I say that we must talk to ourselves instead of allowing ourselves to talk to us.... Have you realized that most of your unhappiness in life is due to the fact that you are listening to yourself instead of talking to yourself?" Speaking here to those who are prone to depression, he

---

[161] I am not saying here that the flesh (as defined in the concept of fallen sin nature) is the cause of clinical depression, which often has physiological and even genetic roots—merely that the flesh as fallen sin nature can feed into depression, if one responds to the depression in the wrong manner. In the phrase "thorn in the flesh" above, I believe the word *flesh* denotes the physical body (weakened and imperfect as it is in all people through The Fall), not the sin nature. Clinical depression is more than simple negativity in outlook. It can be manifested as a profound, intractable sadness, that no attempt at redirecting the thoughts can completely assuage. While it is impossible to completely and finally rid oneself of depression by simply deciding to be less negative, I believe one can manage it through the practice of "taking one's soul in-hand" that Lloyd-Jones presents. In our resurrected, glorified bodies, we are promised that we will have no depression.

says, "You have to take yourself in-hand, you have to address yourself, preach to yourself, question yourself. You must say to your soul, 'Why art thou cast down—what business have you to be disquieted [alluding here to Psalms 42-43]?" He continues, "And then you must go on to remind yourself of God, Who God is, and what God is and what God has done, and what God has pledged Himself to do."[162] In Philippians 4:7, 9 we find that God has pledged Himself to give us His peace when we practice these things. And in that process, I am able to dwell in Him.

Dane Ortlund concludes his wonderful book *Gentle and Lowly* with the following admonition:

> Whatever is crumbling all around you in your life, wherever you feel stuck this remains, undeflectable: his heart for you, the real you, is gentle and lowly. So go to him. That place in your life where you feel most defeated, he is there; he lives there, right there, and his heart for you, not on the other side of it but in that darkness, is gentle and lowly. Your anguish is his home. Go to him. (Ortlund 216)

Hopelessness, anguish, despair, defeat, the feeling of being overwhelmed by life—those are the very places where He meets us! We are not to think we have to conquer and clean up these areas on our own. In those very places, we may step under the shelter of His wings in repentance to dwell there, and allow Him to be our God, a God of deliverances. A God who leads us to let the day's own trouble be sufficient for the day. A God who is unmistakably in control of the world. A God of unlimited lovingkindness and mercies. "His mercies never come to an end; they are new every morning" (Lamentations 3:22-23). And we have the consolation

---

[162] D. Martyn Lloyd-Jones, *Spiritual Depression: Its Causes and Its Cure* (Grand Rapids, MI: WM. B. Eerdmans Publishing Co., 1965), p. 21.

that our trials and difficulties now are producing an "eternal weight of glory" in the life to come:

> But we have this treasure in earthen vessels, so that the surpassing greatness of the power will be of God and not from ourselves.... Therefore, we do not lose heart, but though our outer man is decaying, yet our inner man is being renewed day by day. For momentary, light affliction is producing for us an eternal weight of glory far beyond all comparison, while we look not at the things which are seen, but at the things which are not seen; for the things which are seen are temporal, but the things which are not seen are eternal. (II Corinthians 4:7, 16-18)

So, if I may ask, where are **you** in this process? I'm quite certain that many of you are further along than I am. But then again, might some of you also be stuck in some cave needing rescue, as David was? If so, cry out to God as David did in Psalms 142 (refer to **Chapter 4** for more on waiting). You may want to also try, as I have done, thinking back over each of the activities of one who dwells (abiding, waiting, resting, praying, worshipping, studying, meditating and walking) and doing a personal inventory. In so doing, please remember that God has taken up personal residence in your heart if you are a believer, and that He will never forsake you. He is more concerned about where your heart is right now than any less-than-perfect track record (and none of us will ever have a perfect track record except the LORD Jesus). I hope this book has helped give you some better idea about how to continue, or to begin, growing as "one who dwells."

For Further Thought:

1. Where am I dwelling most of the time: in the world, in my problems, or in Christ? What does my mind dwell upon when

I am not focused upon some particular problem or issue at hand? What does my mind default to?

2. What is the orientation of my heart towards God right now? Do I regularly enjoy times of Bible study and prayer, or have those activities become just other responsibilities or possibly even drudgeries?

3. Have I ever really learned to wait and rest on God? What, specifically, am I waiting on God for, and when was the last time I recognized true peace and rest in Him?

4. The five greatest hindrances in **dwelling** with God, as discussed in **Chapter 1.3**, are idols, busyness, Biblical illiteracy, negativity and legalism. If we were to consider what may be the greatest hindrances in consistently practicing these eight disciplines, habits or activities, sure enough these same five hindrances would be reflected in our list:

Habits and Hindrances

Waiting	Impatience (**busyness**), being unaware of God's specific promises to embrace (**Biblical illiteracy**), lack of faith in His promises
Praying/ Worshipping	Discouragement, lack of personal discipline, being too self-absorbed (**idols**), being overwhelmed (one solution is to break prayer list into smaller segments), **busyness, negativity**
Resting	**Legalism, busyness,** lack of faith, lacking knowledge of God's greatness, love and specific promises (**Biblical illiteracy**) such as Matthew 11:28-30, not living in "day-tight increments" (Matthew 6:34)
Studying	Aversion to reading and studying in general (these are skills that must be learned and practiced), misunderstanding over the role our minds must play in the process of Bible study (**Biblical illiteracy**), digital distractions, **busyness**
Meditating	Misunderstanding what true Biblical meditation is (it will always involve His Word—therefore, **Biblical illiteracy** would be a hindrance), **busyness,** digital distractions, **negativity**
Walking	Walking with the world or the flesh instead of with Christ (as with **idols**, I John 2:15-16), complacency, stumbling through each day without making time to focus upon the LORD through His Word and prayer (**busyness**)

What has been my personal experience in regard to each of these hindrances? Have I encountered others not listed? What are some practical steps I might undertake to overcome each of these hindrances? (See Ephesians 5:15-16.) For example, to overcome the hindrances to prayer and Bible study, I might determine to have my devotional each morning **before** I turn on my phone or my laptop; or to overcome the hindrances to meditating, I might begin a Scripture memory program.

Suggested Memory Verses:

Dwell

He who **dwells** in the shelter of the Most High
Will abide in the shadow of the Almighty. (Psalms 91:1)

Abide

If you **abide** in Me, and My words **abide** in you, ask whatever you wish, and it will be done for you. (John 15:7)

Wait

Wait for the Lord;
Be strong and let your heart take courage;
Yes, **wait** for the Lord. (Psalms 27:14)

Pray

Rejoice always; **pray** without ceasing; in everything give thanks; for this is God's will for you in Christ Jesus. (I Thessalonians 5:16-18)

Be anxious for nothing, but in everything by **prayer** and supplication with thanksgiving let your requests be made known to God. And the peace of God, which surpasses all comprehension, will guard your hearts and your minds in Christ Jesus. (Philippians 4:6-7)

Rest

"Come to Me, all who are weary and heavy-laden, and I will give you **rest**. Take My yoke upon you and learn from Me, for I am gentle and humble in heart, and you will find **rest** for your souls. For My yoke is easy and My burden is light." (Matthew 11:28-30)

Study

Study to shew thyself approved unto God, a workman that needeth not to be ashamed, rightly dividing the word of truth. (II Timothy 2:15, KJV)

Meditate

This book of the law shall not depart from your mouth, but you shall **meditate** on it day and night, so that you may be careful to do according to all that is written in it; for then you will make your way prosperous, and then you will have success. (Joshua 1:8)

How blessed is the man who does not walk in the counsel of the wicked,
Nor stand in the path of sinners,
Nor sit in the seat of scoffers!
But his delight is in the law of the Lord,
And in His law he **meditates** day and night.
He will be like a tree *firmly* planted by streams of water,
Which yields its fruit in its season
And its leaf does not wither;
And in whatever he does, he prospers. (Psalms 1:1-3)

Walk

Therefore I, the prisoner of the Lord, implore you to **walk** in a manner worthy of the calling with which you have been called, with all humility and gentleness, with patience, showing tolerance for one another in love, being diligent to preserve the unity of the Spirit in the bond of peace. (Ephesians 4:1-3)

Therefore be careful how you **walk**, not as unwise men but as wise, making the most of your time, because the days are evil. (Ephesians 5:15-16)

And Finally, from the Account of the Apostle Paul's Experience in Dwelling

I have fought the good fight, I have finished the course, I have kept the faith; in the future there is laid up for me the crown of righteousness, which the Lord, the righteous Judge, will award to me on that day; and not only to me, but also to all who have loved His appearing. (II Timothy 4:7-8)

Afterword

This morning, our dog Rikki gave me the perfect lesson on dwelling. As I was looking for Sara, it occurred to me where I might find her. Sure enough, she was having her quiet time in her special place and was there on her knees in prayer when I looked in. There behind her, asleep on the floor, was Rikki, the picture of contentment. Rikki LOVES Sara; me he tolerates. Each evening Sara invites Rikki up into her lap (this dog weighs over 40 pounds!), and pampers him by scratching his chest, ears and back. She has a special, tender tone of voice when she speaks to him. Whenever Rikki hears her voice call his name, he instantly hustles to her side. In her presence there is fullness of joy for Rikki, and in her right hand are pleasures forevermore (i.e., Beggin' Strips), as it says in Psalms 16. Rikki was content this morning because he was in the presence of someone who genuinely loved him, and he knew it, someone who always had his best interests at heart. He trusted her, his master. Sara commented that as believers we can have that same kind of relationship with our very own "Abba Father," and that relationship is verified by the time we devote to seeking His face and dwelling in His presence. She went on to comment, "You'll never want to dwell with God until you know Who He is." How true! I hope this book has helped you see Him more clearly. When Jesus taught his disciples to pray in Matthew 6, he instructed them to address their Heavenly Father quite literally as "Daddy" (verse 9). Can you comprehend the tenderness in that? In Psalms 27, David says,

One thing I have asked from the Lord, that I shall seek: That I may **dwell** in the house of the Lord all the days of my

life,
To **behold the beauty of the Lord**
And to **meditate** in His temple.

What does it mean for us to "behold the beauty of the Lord?" This side of the cross, we don't **have** a temple to go to; we **are** the temple! God is able to dwell in us because of what He did through Jesus on the cross. We need never fear His righteous wrath again. Therein lies His beauty—He is actively pursuing us so we can enjoy that kind of contentment and **rest** in a relationship with Him—so that we can **dwell** in Him. The God who spoke the stars into existence and Who now controls the entire universe has a special tenderness reserved for you and for me! He knows our names,[163] and He calls them out in that tenderness. We can find true contentment, true **rest**, in His presence (**our true home**) because of the confidence we can place in Him, based on what we know about Him through His Word (Hebrews 10:9-25). That is especially important during these trying times.

I began putting my thoughts together for this book before the coronavirus became a pandemic. It never occurred to me at that time how relevant the topic might become to those seeking refuge in God from such a crisis, but such is now the case. That crisis has dramatically changed the everyday lives of billions of people. I have noticed the increasing popularity of, and frequency of references to, Psalms 91 during this time. This psalm contains some remarkable promises for "He who dwells" (verse 1). The one who dwells in Christ as a refuge is then addressed as "you" throughout the remainder of the psalm. Verses 5-12 may seem at

---

[163] See Psalms 139:1-6, John 10:27-28 and Exodus 33:17, wherein God addresses Moses and tells him He knows Moses' name.

first glance to make an unqualified promise of protection to this person:

> You will not be afraid of the terror by night,
> Or of the arrow that flies by day;
> ⁶Of the **pestilence** that stalks in darkness,
> Or of the destruction that lays waste at noon.
> ⁷**A thousand may fall at your side**
> **And ten thousand at your right hand,**
> ***But* it shall not approach you.**
> ⁸You will only look on with your eyes
> And see the recompense of the wicked.
> ⁹**For you have made the Lord, my refuge,**
> ***Even* the Most High, your dwelling place.**
> ¹⁰No evil will befall you,
> Nor will any **plague** come near your tent.
>
> ¹¹For He will give His angels charge concerning you,
> To guard you in all your ways.
> ¹²They will bear you up in their hands,
> That you do not strike your foot against a stone.

It must be remembered, however, that Satan tried to tempt Christ into jumping from the roof of the temple in order to flaunt His special status before God. He did this by quoting verses 11 and 12 of this very passage. The angels would bear Him up, Satan assured Him. In doing this Satan twisted the Scripture from its **authorial intent**, and Jesus corrected him by **correlating** those verses with Deuteronomy 6:16: "You shall not put the Lord your God to the test..." I fear that some Christians in our world today may have falsely used such scriptures as Psalms 91 to reassure themselves that they are divinely immune from this virus, even to the point of disregarding common-sense precautions, some even flaunting their disregard for the guidelines. We might also **correlate**

Proverbs 22:3 here—"The prudent sees the evil and hides himself, / But the naive go on, and are punished for it." Then, on the other hand, there are verses such as Hebrews 10:24-25, which says, "…and let us consider how to stimulate one another to love and good deeds, **not forsaking our own assembling together**, as is the habit of some, but encouraging *one another*; and all the more as you see the day drawing near," and there are times when we are called upon to leave our own comfort zones to step out in faith and serve the LORD. So, the leadership of each church must bring all of this before the LORD "in fear and trembling" (Philippians 2:12) so as to choose the right path, and circumstances may vary for each individual believer (some being at higher risk than others) in determining which is the correct path to take. If I may also use here a piece of Scripture that was applied in its original context to financial giving, but in which the same principle might apply in this context, II Corinthians 9:7 states, "Each one *must do* just as he has purposed in his [own] heart, not grudgingly or under compulsion, for God loves a cheerful giver." As we have seen in **Chapter 6**, "one who dwells" is careful to ensure a sound **interpretation** of Scripture before making any **application**, thereby "rightly handling the Word of truth" (II Timothy 2:15). The Scriptures are able to discern, or judge, the thoughts and intentions of our hearts in any applications we might want to make (Hebrews 4:12). As I read the Scriptures, we are to love the LORD with all our minds and hearts (Matthew 22:37). We talked about **double-mindedness** and **integrity** in **Chapter 1.2**, with integrity being the key prerequisite for dwelling in Christ. Our constant prayer should be:

Search me, O God, and **know my heart**;
Try me and know my anxious thoughts;
And see if there be any hurtful way in me,
And lead me in the everlasting way. (Psalms 139:23-24)

Prayer is the one discipline I most need to improve on—specifically the focused, intentional, systematic, intercessory type of prayer (using a list)—but may it never become for me a legalistic exercise! I'm thankful that my LORD is not impressed with my "many words" when I pray (Matthew 6:7). He is more concerned with the position of my heart. In **Chapter 2**, we saw how prayer is a key tool God can use in getting us "unstuck" or "un-burdened." And we must always remember that the God we pray to is completely, **meticulously in control** at all times. He has, however, ordained that our prayers are the instrument He frequently uses to bring His will to pass. It could be far too easy for us to become burdened by the seemingly overwhelming responsibility to **abide, wait, pray, worship, rest, study, meditate and walk,** if we forget that these activities or disciplines are ones the Holy Spirit will, Himself, guide us into and build into our lives as we dwell, and that to dwell we need simply to seek His face in all things. As David says,

> Hear, O Lord, when I cry with my voice,
> And be gracious to me and answer me.
> *When You said,* "Seek My face," my heart said to You,
> "Your face, O Lord, I shall seek."
> Do not hide Your face from me…. (Psalms 27:7-9a)

I seriously doubt that David felt the need to use a checklist with all of these disciplines written on it, and yet we see him practicing all of them because he was seeking God's face to dwell with Him. That means his heart was undivided (that is, he had **integrity**) in his pursuit of fellowship with God, and God then led him to **pray**, to **meditate** on the scriptures, to **wait** on God, and even to **rest**. That's what it means to **dwell** with the LORD, and that's the type of **walk** I want to have with Him. How about you?

From Moses' final prayer for Israel:

The eternal God is a dwelling place,
And underneath are the everlasting arms... (Deuteronomy
33:27a)

As a concluding doxology, please allow me to leave you with the chorus and final stanza of a beautiful hymn based on Psalms 91, recently written and composed by Keith Getty et. al., and performed by Keith and Kristyn Getty, entitled "My Dwelling Place:"[164]

Wonderful, powerful
My hope and my defender
Mighty God, Emmanuel
My dwelling place forever

My dwelling place is God Most High
I'll never seek another
For I am His and He is mine
My heart He'll keep forever
I know the Name on Whom I call
He promises to answer
With life He satisfies my soul
And crowns me with His pleasure

---

[164] Words and music by Keith Getty, Kristyn Getty, Kelly Minter, Chris Eaton and Stuart Townend. 2016, 2018 Getty Music Publishing (BMI) / Getty Music Songs, LLC (adm. by MusicServices.org) / Here's to JO (BMI) / West Lodge Music (BMI) (adm. by BMG) / Townend Songs (PRS) (adm. by MusicServices.org in the US and Canada and by songsolutions.org elsewhere in the world). <gettymusic.com/mydwellingplace>

Index of Appendices

Appendix 1

Studies of the Words *Dwell* and *Abide*

Sources for the following material:

Kenneth S. Wuest. *Wuest's Word Studies: Studies in the Vocabulary of the Greek New Testament for the English Reader.* Grand Rapids, MI: Wm. B. Eerdmans Publishing Co., 1945 (Ninth Printing, 1971), pp. 63-65.

W.E. Vine. *An Expository Dictionary of New Testament Words: with their Precise Meanings for English Readers.* Old Tappan, New Jersey: Fleming H. Revel Company, 1940 (Seventeenth Impression, 1966), pp. 10-11, 344-346.

Analysis: Vine identifies 14 different verbs that translate into "dwell." The majority have as their root the Greek word transliterated as <u>Oikeo</u> (pronounced oi-keh'-oh), which is from the noun *oikos,* meaning "house." The root meaning of the verb is, therefore, to inhabit as one's abode, i.e. to reside permanently, as in a house. This word is used with the indwelling of the Holy Spirit in believers. The second most common root is *skenoo* (pronounced skeh-nah'-oh), which means to pitch a tent (or to live in a tent, as Wuest has it), or to tabernacle. This was John's preferred word for this general concept. This verb is used in John

1:14, which may then be translated as "The Word became flesh and *tabernacled* among us." This paints a beautiful picture—that we have in Christ everything the Israelites had in their tabernacle in the wilderness, which was actually just a picture of what Christ would later become more fully for us. It may readily be seen that the Old Testament tabernacle, and later Christ's earthly, unglorified body, were temporary manifestations; although, Christ will maintain His glorified body through eternity. The third most common root word translated as "dwell" in Vine is the word transliterated as *meno*. This word means to "abide" or "remain." Vine finds this word translated as *dwell* seven times in the New Testament, six in John and once in Acts. Elsewhere, it is translated as *abide*. It may be used of place, of time or of qualities. Vine identifies six different Greek words with this root, all translated as *abide*. Wuest, however, has a different take on this word *abide* altogether:

> This is one of John's favorite words…. The word therefore has the ideas of "permanence of position, occupying a place as one's dwelling place, holding and maintaining unbroken communion and fellowship with another." (Wuest 64-65)

It is interesting that he employs the word "dwell" (as in *dwelling* place) to define the word "abide." Wuest's comments on the word "dwell" are limited to its translation from the root *skenoo*. No other roots are considered. His entire commentary is one paragraph only.

Conclusion: I must go with Vine on the meanings of these two words, if for no other reason than the contrast in the thoroughness of their analyses. *Dwell* carries more the idea of permanence in a literal or figurative place (particularly when its root is *oikos*), while *abide* emphasizes the vital connection that exists (as in the vine of

John 15), irrespective of a place (literal or figurative) being involved. *Dwell*, therefore, has a broader meaning than *abide*.

In the Old Testament, the Hebrew word transliterated as *yashab* (Strong's number 3427) is the word primarily translated as *dwell*. According to Biblestudytools.com, the word could possibly also mean remain, sit or abide. <https://www.biblestudytools.com/lexicons/hebrew/nas/yashab.html>

Appendix 2

A Myopic Manifesto
"Crossing Those Bridges When We Get There."

Now, therefore, without the slightest hesitation, we will presume to speak for the entire worldwide Myopic Community in establishing this as our common Manifesto and Creed.

Manifesto: It is our full intention at this particular moment to live the rest of our lives entirely for the moment, while defending and celebrating Myopia as a legitimate and respectable lifestyle.

Simply stated, Myopia is a celebration of action in advance of thought. As everyone knows, serious reflection can at times become troubling and inhibiting. The Myopic impulse, on the other hand, bubbles up from the Divine Inner Child inside each of us. Since in reality there is no ultimate purpose to our existence, every impulse is equally legitimate, as long as it is sanctioned by The Herd. Anyone can merely look at The Herd out there today and recognize that they are all surely onto something. The challenge for each individual, therefore, lies in shoving one's way out to the front and staying there. There is an Elite Group at the head of The Herd that lives in a state of perfect self-actualization. We know this on the authority of television itself. Those who lag behind may never share the lofty camaraderie of the current Elite leaders of The Herd.

Our Creed is simple: If you encounter a laggard, run over him. There is a proper place for traditional civility, but it is always in the clubhouse after the game has been won and the bets paid. While in the frenzied heat of imitation, never take your eyes off the butts of the Elite. Try to stay right behind them, and slam on your brakes whenever they do. There is shame only in inaction and indecisiveness. Disdain moralizing in any form, except that which champions competitive drive and self-confidence. Any action can be justified before The Herd if it is argued with enough force and self-assurance, The Herd's true spirit. Keep your friends freshly culled. Associate only with those who confirm your beliefs, or with those whose conflicting ideas you may easily overwhelm through bluster or intimidation. Never let up. Faster is always better. More is always best. Be there. Do that. Seek driving excitement. Seize every moment and then crush it!

The current groundswell of enthusiasm for Myopic living is attracting increasing numbers each year. All who feel oppressed under the brutal strictures of common sense should join today before thinking better of it. Local representatives are readily identifiable.

[Satire by Bob Cofield, All Rights Reserved]

Appendix 3

The Covenants and the Prophecies—How and When They Will Be Fulfilled

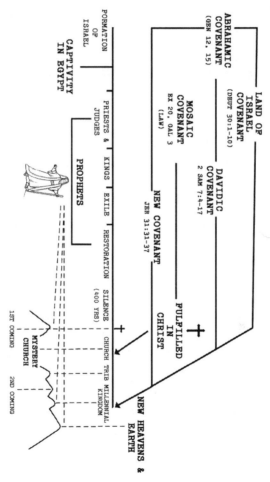

Appendix 3 is adapted from Tim LaHaye and Thomas Ice, *Charting the End Times* (Eugene, OR: Harvest House Publishers,

cont.next page

2001), p. 80. Used by permission. Theirs, in turn, was adapted from Paul Benware, *Understanding End Time Prophecy: A Comprehensive Approach* (Chicago: Moody Press, 1995), p. 50.

It should first be noted that this entire diagram is actually one long timeline. On the far left is the formation of Israel. As time progresses, we move to the right, culminating in the Millennial Kingdom (a thousand-year period following Christ's Second Coming during which He will reign from Jerusalem) followed by the new heavens and the new earth, at which time in the future God will be able to perfectly **dwell** among His people (at that point consisting of both the Church and those from the House of Israel who have accepted Christ). Appendix 4 provides more detail about the entire sequence of events in the End Times.

All of Israel is descended from Abraham (and through Christ, we [the Church] are also, according to Galatians 3:29, his spiritual descendants). As our pastor often reminds us, God gave three promises to Abraham: (1) Lots of land—**The Land of Israel Covenant** (Deuteronomy 30: 1-10), (2) Lots of people (Abraham's descendants would be vast in number and one of them would rule as king on earth [King David—**The Davidic Covenant**], **and his** throne would be established forever [II Samuel 7:4-17]) and (3) A blessing would come through Abraham's Descendant (Christ). God would provide a world-wide blessing—the means for spiritual regeneration—though Christ. Jesus says in John 4:22 that "salvation is from the Jews." This latter covenant (**The New Covenant** in Jeremiah 31:33-37) has been partially fulfilled in the Church of today and will include the whole house of Israel in the

Millennial Kingdom and the new heavens and new earth. **The Land of Israel Covenant** has been only partially fulfilled today, and of course, **The Davidic Covenant** will be fulfilled in the millennial reign of Christ, who as David's descendant will reign forever.

The Mosaic Covenant was the Law given to Moses at Mount Sinai. Its requirements were completely fulfilled in Christ through his sinless life and his crucifixion in our place, followed by His resurrection. When we are saved His righteousness is imputed to us. Refer to Appendix 9 for more about the theology of salvation. In Galatians 3:24, the Apostle Paul explains how the Law reveals our need for a Savior because we are unable to fulfill its requirements: "Therefore the Law has become our tutor *to lead us* to Christ, so that we may be justified by faith."

Notice in the diagram how all of the lines (covenants) converge for their fulfillment on the End Times, which arguably begin with the **Church Age**. Again, see Appendix 4 for more detail about the End Times. The Church Age was a mystery to the prophets as they viewed the future through the inspired lens of their own prophecies. The **Church Age** is, therefore, depicted in the diagram as being a hidden valley between the two mountain peaks of the first and second comings, not in view of the prophets. They could see the mountain peaks but not the hidden valley between. This was part of the reason why the Jewish people did not recognize Jesus as being their Messiah when he came. He came the first time as a suffering servant (see Isaiah 53), and the second time he will come as a reigning king (see Isaiah 9:6-7, Daniel 7:13-14 and

Revelation 19). How could the same Messiah be both? Both are foretold in the Scriptures. The prophets did not understand completely what their own prophecies meant. Peter, writing to the Church, said the following:

> As to this salvation, the prophets who prophesied of the grace that *would come* to you made careful searches and inquiries, seeking to know what person or time the Spirit of Christ within them was indicating as He predicted the sufferings of Christ and the glories to follow. It was revealed to them that they were not serving themselves, but you, in these things which now have been announced to you through those who preached the gospel to you by the Holy Spirit sent from heaven—things into which angels long to look. (I Peter 1:10-12)

Please keep in mind as you study this diagram that the whole point is to illustrate how our Heavenly Father has been pursuing us, as His people, working through history to restore our fellowship, our **dwelling** with Him, since the time that was lost in the Garden of Eden. All of His efforts are consummated in Christ; now we may **dwell** with Him spiritually and then, once again, face-to-face.

> For we know in part and we prophesy in part; but when the perfect comes, the partial will be done away. When I was a child, I used to speak like a child, think like a child, reason like a child; when I became a man, I did away with childish things. For now we see in a mirror dimly, but then face to

face; now I know in part, but then I will know fully just as I also have been fully known. (I Corinthians 13:9-12)

Appendix 4

The Pre-Millennial Scheme of Events for the End Times

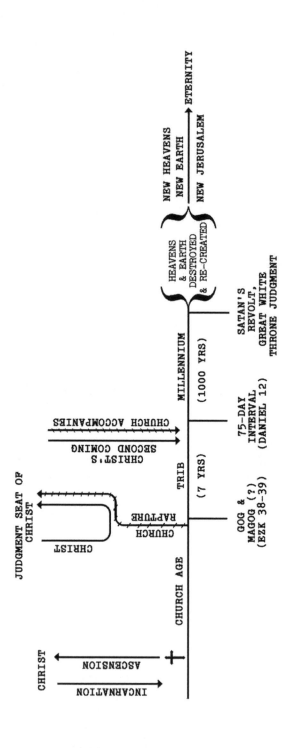

Appendix 5

Dwelling as a Church

While dwelling in Christ must always be first and foremost an individual undertaking, it is never completed in isolation; for obedience to Christ will lead each of us to follow Him into His work through His body, the Church. We are incomplete without this, because each spiritual gift in the Church is given for the purpose of edifying the body.

> ...but speaking the truth in love, we are to grow up in all *aspects* into Him who is the head, *even* Christ, from whom the whole body, being fitted and held together by what every joint supplies, according to the proper working of each individual part, causes the growth of the body for the building up of itself in love. (Ephesians 4:15-16)

I Corinthians 3:16 tells us that Christ dwells in the whole church collectively, in addition to indwelling each believer:

> Do you not know that you [here referring to the whole Church] are a temple of God and *that* the Spirit of God dwells in you?

This is further clarified in Ephesians 2:19-22:

So then you are no longer strangers and aliens, but you are fellow citizens with the saints, and are of God's household, having been built on the foundation of the apostles and prophets, Christ Jesus Himself being the corner *stone*, in whom the whole building, being fitted together, is growing into a holy temple in the Lord, in whom **you also are being built together into a dwelling of God in the Spirit.**

Speaking to an entire church (at Laodicea) that had become lukewarm in its spiritual life, the resurrected Jesus says in Revelation 3:20, "Behold, I stand at the door and knock; if anyone hears My voice and opens the door, I will come in to him and will dine with him, and he with Me." That's a powerful image of intimacy and dwelling with Him.

It's a team sport! I would go so far as to say that anyone seeking to dwell in Christ who is not involved in a local church is lacking something fundamental, and is obviously not reading the same Bible I am. So how can the Church be unified in this effort to foster dwelling by each of its members? I believe it must begin with the church staff, elders and/or deacons and extend from there to every member. There must be a unity and a mutual edification process in play. I see this intergenerational interaction happening in the church I attend. The young people have stepped in to fill the absence of some older members because of COVID concerns. There is also intergenerational participation in missionary activities. Several adults who have no children of their own in the youth program are involved in it themselves. We have seen the Lord bless these efforts in our church. Elsewhere, however, it could be easy for the older members to feel disconnected from the younger ones and vice-versa (particularly because of the digital disconnect that exists for most elderly people). Nationally, one third of adults aged sixty-five or older say they've never used the

Internet, and half say they don't have Internet access at home.[165] (Thankfully, this is not the case in our church.) This is so crucial in other churches because of the social isolation of many of the older members, and because of the tremendous onslaught of counter-Christian cultural influences bombarding our youth today. Nationally, **approximately two-thirds of churchgoing young people will have lost their faith by the end of their first year in college.**[166] Please allow that fact to soak in.

Barna Group researchers David Kinnaman and Mark Matlock have looked closely at the spiritual lives of eighteen- to twenty-nine-year-olds ("Millennials") with a churchgoing background, to determine why those in that category who maintained a resilient faith continue doing so.[167] Their study distinguished four kinds of exiles:[168] Prodigals (Ex-Christians, 22%), Nomads (Unchurched, 30%), Habitual Churchgoers (38%), and **Resilient Disciples (10%).** The last category is defined by four behaviors:[169]

- Attend church at least monthly, and engage with their church more than just attending worship services

---

[165] Fields, Jessica, "We are leaving older adults out of the digital world." TechCrunch, 5 May 2019. Accessed 26 August 2020. <https://techcrunch.com/2019/05/05/we-are-leaving-older-adults-out-of-the-digital-world/>

[166] "Most Teenagers Drop Out of Church as Young Adults," Lifeway Research. 15 January 2019. Accessed 25 August 2020. <https://lifewayresearch.com/2019/01/15/most-teenagers-drop-out-of-church-as-young-adults/>

[167] Kinnaman, David and Mark Matlock. *Faith for Exiles: 5 Ways for a New Generation to follow Jesus in Digital Babylon.* Grand Rapids, MI, Baker Books, 2019.

[168] His term for people living in culture he defines as "Digital Babylon." Refer to discussion in **Chapter 2** for more insight on this concept.

[169] Ibid., p. 33.

- Trust firmly in the authority of the Bible

- Are committed to Jesus personally and affirm His death, burial and resurrection to conquer sin and death

- Express a desire to transform the broader society as an outcome of their faith

The five practices that keep this group spiritually healthy include the following (emphasized are the items related specifically to dwelling and intergenerational interaction):[170]

- **Form resilient identity by experiencing intimacy with Jesus.**

- In a complex and anxious age, develop the muscles of cultural discernment. [To this I would add participate in a thorough and comprehensive apologetics program.]

- When isolation and mistrust are norms, **form meaningful, intergenerational relationships.**

- Train for vocational discipleship in various careers.

- Curb entitlement and self-interest tendencies by engaging in countercultural mission.

The report goes on to say that "The vast majority of resilient disciples firmly assert that 'the church is a place where I feel I belong' (88%) and 'I am connected to a community of Christians' (82%)."[171]

---

[170] Ibid., pp. 34-35. "Think of these as the spiritual scaffolding around a young soul that enables the Holy Spirit to access the life inside…"

[171] "Strong Relationships Within Church Add to Resilient Faith in Young Adults." Barna.org. August 26, 2020. Accessed August 26, 2020. <https://www.barna.com/research/relationships-build-resilient-faith/>

So, the research confirms that a healthy church is one in which Christ's indwelling presence is known by each believer, each believer is interconnected within the body, and that this is not just limited to his or her own demographic. Kinnaman and Matlock have concluded that the pandemic will only accelerate the loss of young people from the church, unless more intergenerational connectedness is established soon.[172]

---

[172] "Will the 2020 Pandemic Accelerate Loss of Faith Among the Next Generation?" Barna Group, 2020. Barna.org , 6 October 2020. <https://www.barna.com/research/pandemic-accelerate-loss-aith/>

Appendix 6

"Light Shining Out of Darkness"

By William Cowper (1773)

(First published by John Newton, slave-trader turned Abolitionist and author of "Amazing Grace." Retrieved from the public domain.)

God moves in a mysterious way,
  His wonders to perform;
He plants his footsteps in the sea,
  And rides upon the storm.

Deep in unfathomable mines
  Of never failing skill;
He treasures up his bright designs,
  And works His sovereign will.

Ye fearful saints fresh courage take,
  The clouds ye so much dread
Are big with mercy, and shall break
  In blessings on your head.

Judge not the Lord by feeble sense,
But trust him for his grace;
Behind a frowning providence,
He hides a smiling face.

His purposes will ripen fast,
Unfolding ev'ry hour;
The bud may have a bitter taste,
But sweet will be the flow'r.

Blind unbelief is sure to err,
And scan his work in vain;
God is his own interpreter,
And he will make it plain.

Appendix 7

"Be Still, My Soul"

Be still, my soul: The Lord is on thy side;
With patience bear thy cross of grief or pain.
Leave to thy God to order and provide;
In ev'ry change he faithful will remain.
Be still, my soul: Thy best, thy heav'nly Friend
Thru thorny ways leads to a joyful end.

Be still, my soul: Thy God doth undertake
To guide the future as he has the past.
Thy hope, thy confidence let nothing shake;
All now mysterious shall be bright at last.
Be still, my soul: The waves and winds still know
His voice who ruled them while he dwelt below.

Be still, my soul: The hour is hast'ning on
When we shall be forever with the Lord,
When disappointment, grief, and fear are gone,
Sorrow forgot, love's purest joys restored.
Be still, my soul: When change and tears are past,
All safe and blessed we shall meet at last.

'"Be Still, My Soul" was written by German author Katharina Amalia Dorothea von Schlegel in 1752, later translated into English in 1855 by Jane Laurie Borthwick. Retrieved from the public domain.

"The History and Impromptu Performance by David Archuleta March 27, 2014." *The Tabernacle Choir Blog.* The Church of Jesus Christ of Latter-Day Saints. 29 September 2020. <https://www.thetabernaclechoir.org/articles/be-still-my-soul-david-archueta.html>. As explained in **Chapter 4**, the lyrics of this great hymn speak beautifully to the issue of God's sovereignty and providence, and of praying to and trusting Him when our impulse is to fret, worry and despair. I kept these lyrics taped beside my computer screen while I was teaching school, and since I have retired, they have been posted in my study.

Appendix 8

Thistle

Then to Adam He said, "Because you have listened to the voice of your wife, and have eaten from the tree about which I commanded you, saying, 'You shall not eat from it';

Cursed is the ground because of you;
With hard labor you shall eat from it
All the days of your life.
Both thorns and thistles it shall grow for you;
Yet you shall eat the plants of the field;

By the sweat of your face
You shall eat bread,
Until you return to the ground,
Because from it you were taken;
For you are dust,
And to dust you shall return. (Genesis 3:17-19)

But He said to them, "I have food to eat that you do not know of…. My food is to do the will of Him who sent me and to accomplish His work." (John 4:32, 34)

* * *

My gnarly knees do some days pop in protest
like the windshield wipers of my aging truck
that someone vandalized in the high-school parking lot,
twisting their mechanical gristle
from its intended form.
I want to think it was just a random act
from a student grown weary
of crushing candy or watching birds dodge missiles and explode.
Please say it was not the English language I extolled these many weeks,
and say it was not something I said or did amiss
or even failed to say or do, but should have.
Say, rather, it was a thorn to humble me,
a thistle in the garden I till
by the sweat of my face.
I could live well-contented with that,
though the used mechanical tiller I bought "as is"—
the one that would not crank when I brought it home—
also wanted sweat.
And sweat I gave to it,
each lever, spring, bell and whistle.
Tell me, in what other time or place
could I raise so rich a harvest?

Appendix 9

Part I: Understanding and Explaining the Gospel

Biblical Principles:

1. <u>Our preparation and motives</u>: Fishers of men (Matthew 4:19), As we go (Matthew 28:19-20) ask, "Where is God already working?" (John 5:17), Be prepared to make a defense (I Peter 3:15), Study to...rightly handle Word (II Timothy 2:15), Not ashamed of gospel (Romans 1:16).

2. <u>Spiritual discernment</u>: Where is this person spiritually? (I Thessalonians 5:14—witness to, exhort, encourage, confront, instruct, or even learn from?) Questions or objections? The unrighteous suppress the truth (Romans 1:18), I Corinthians 2:2-13—discernment needed.

3. <u>Regeneration</u> ("new birth") is completely a work of God (John 6:29, 44; 10:27-30).

4. <u>Conversion</u> = Repentance + Faith (Acts 20:21) "Repentance is a heartfelt sorrow for sin, a renouncing of it, and a sincere commitment to forsake it and walk in obedience to Christ" (Wayne Grudem, Systematic Theology, Page 713).

5. <u>God uses His Spirit (John 3:5-6), His word (Romans 10:17)
   and His people (Romans 10:14-15)</u> in this process. We can
   then become His ambassadors (II Corinthians 5:18-20).

6. <u>Man cannot save himself</u>. Living a "Christian life" will not
   save (Matthew 7:21-13). A "believers' prayer," walking the
   aisle, raising a hand, or looking up at the preacher does not
   save anyone. Even belief in the facts of the gospel saves no
   one ("the demons also believe and shudder"—James 2:19-
   20). Baptism will not save you. Repentance and faith, alone,
   save, and these must be accomplished by God working in the
   sinner, and they involve a personal response from the sinner.
   The gospel is the good news that God is able to reconcile
   people unto Himself through Christ, and that He offers this
   as a gift.

The Bridge:

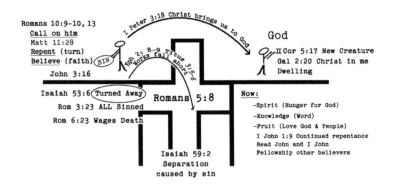

The Romans Road:

<u>3:23</u>—All have sinned and fall short of the glory of God

<u>6:23</u>—The wages of sin is death, but the gift of God is eternal life through Christ

<u>5:8</u>—God shows his love for us in that while we were yet sinners, Christ died for us

<u>10:9</u>—If you confess with your mouth the Lord Jesus and believe in your heart that God raised him from the dead, you will be saved (10:13—everyone who calls on the name of the Lord will be saved)

<u>5:1</u>—Therefore, since we have been justified through faith, we have peace through our Lord Jesus Christ

<u>8:38-39</u>—[Nothing]…can separate us from the Love of God that is in Christ Jesus our Lord

The Gospel Explained, Part II (The Theology of Salvation)

SALVATION

	1	2	3	4	5	6	7
	SPIRIT	REGENERATION	INSTANT	PAST	REBORN	LEGAL	INVITE
	SOUL	SANCTIFICATION	LIFETIME	PRESENT	REFORMED	PRACTICAL	WALK
	BODY	GLORIFICATION	INSTANT	FUTURE	TRANSFORMED	PHYSICAL	HOPE

1. Which part of the person involved.
2. Theological label for salvation of this part.
3. How long a period required.
4. When it happens in life of Christian.
5. Result of the process or event.
6. Description of the process or event.
7. The believer's responsibility in each part of salvation.

NOTE: This model should NOT suggest that the body is inherently more evil than the non-physical aspects of man's being. The physical aspect of man's being is valuable and important to God.

NOTE: Be aware that this "Tripartite" or "Trichotomous" conception of the human person is, actually, **MISLEADING** in interpreting **SOME** Bible passages. In some cases, the words soul and spirit are used interchangeably. Also, the word heart sometimes refers to the entire soul, and sometimes to only a portion of it. An alternative view is the "Dichotomous Model." The best defense of this model is found in Wayne Grudem's Systematic Theology (chapter 23). Also, J.P. Moreland's book, Love Your God With All Your Mind (Colorado Springs, CO: NAVPress, 2012) offers a very thoughtful development of the Dichotomous Model (Chapter 3).

A Trichotomous Conception of the Human Person
(I Thessalonians 5:23)

BODY

EMOTIONS
MIND
WILL

"HEART" } SOUL (HEBREWS 4:12)

SPIRIT I Cor 3:16

The Gospel Explained, Part III–Three Kinds of People

The following is adapted from *Have You Made the Wonderful Discovery of the Sprit-Filled Life?* written by Bill Bright, ©1966-2021 Bright Media Foundation and Campus Crusade for Christ Inc. All rights reserved. Used with kind permission. <https://crustore.org/>

In the first of two recorded letters that the Apostle Paul sent to the church in Corinth, he identifies three kinds of people in the world today. Every living person is in one of these three groups. They include:

The **Natural Man:**

> But a **natural man** does not accept the things of the Spirit of God, for they are foolishness to him; and he cannot understand them, because they are spiritually appraised. (I Corinthians 2:14)

The **Spiritual Man:**

> But **he who is spiritual** appraises all things, yet he himself is appraised by no one. For who has known the mind of the Lord, that he will instruct Him? But we have the mind of Christ. (I Corinthians 2:15-16)

And the **Carnal Man:**

> And I, brethren, could not speak to you as to spiritual men, but as to **men of flesh [carnal men]**, as to **infants in Christ**. I gave you milk to drink, not solid food; for you were not yet able *to receive it*. Indeed, even now you are not yet able, for you are still fleshly. For since there is jealousy and strife

among you, are you not fleshly, and are you not walking like mere [**natural**] men? (I Corinthians 3:1-3)

Bill Bright, the founder of Campus Crusade for Christ, International, published a very helpful booklet in 1966 explaining the differences in these three types of people. The booklet contains a diagram including three circles, each representing a different type of life (presented below in the order they appear in Scripture).

Natural (Lost)　　　**Spiritual**　　　**Carnal**

Within each circle, there is the image of a chair. This chair represents the "throne" (or "driver's seat") of that particular life. Whoever sits on that throne controls the life; and it is either Christ, represented by a cross, or it is the person's ego or self, represented by the letter *E*. Of course, Christ sits on the throne of the spiritual life and the ego sits on the thrones of both the natural and carnal lives. The difference between the natural and carnal life is that Christ is on the outside of the natural life altogether, and He is on the inside of the carnal life, but dethroned in place of the ego. Therein lies the genius of this diagram in illustrating how a carnal person may be saved, yet still have the affairs of his or her life in chaos, disorder and sinful behavior patterns displeasing to God, "resulting in discord and frustration." I have used squiggly lines (in place of Bill Bright's smaller circles of various sizes) to illustrate the various affairs of each life (straight lines in the case of the spiritual life). They are ordered in the spiritual life, but disordered in the natural and carnal lives. To use the terminology developed in **Chapters 2** and **3**, we might say that **the spiritual person is both dwelling and abiding; the natural person is neither dwelling nor abiding; and the carnal person is dwelling (that is, seated in the heavenlies with Christ and indwelt [sealed] by the Holy Spirit), yet not abiding in Christ or controlled or empowered by the Holy Spirit.**

Bright is careful, however, to make the following very important point regarding carnal Christians:

> **The individual who professes to be a Christian but who continues to practice sin should realize that he may not be a Christian at all,** according to I John2:3; 3:6,9, Ephesians 5:5…. Some or all of the following traits may characterize the Christian who does not fully trust God: ignorance of his spiritual heritage, unbelief, disobedience, loss of love for God and for others, no desire for Bible study, legalistic attitude, impure thoughts, jealousy, guilt, worry, discouragement, critical spirit, frustration, aimlessness.

It is interesting to correlate the above list with the hindrances to dwelling listed in **Chapter 1** and with the list of the works of the flesh in Galatians 5:19-21:

> Now the deeds of the flesh are evident, which are: immorality, impurity, sensuality, idolatry, sorcery, enmities, strife, jealousy, outbursts of anger, disputes, dissensions, factions, envying, drunkenness, carousing, and things like these, of which I forewarn you, just as I have forewarned you, that those who practice such things will not inherit the kingdom of God.

For one seeking to dwell with God, this all goes back to our earlier discussion of **integrity** in **Chapter 1**. As you may recall, the concept of integrity is the idea of spiritual wholeness or soundness in all parts. It is the idea of being all-in, of holding nothing back, of being single-minded, as opposed to being double-minded in our commitment to Christ and His lordship over us. This is how we all initially come to Christ, and it is how we must daily seek to realign ourselves as it becomes necessary (in accordance with I John 1:9). Bill Bright refers to this as "Spiritual Breathing" (breathing out by confessing our sins in prayer to God, and breathing in by reappropriating the power and fulness of the Holy Spirit). A carnal Christian must therefore be to some degree miserable if indeed he or she truly belongs to Christ. He or she must have an acute awareness that things are not the way they should be, and a homesickness or a deep longing for reconciliation. Should this be completely lacking, then such a person must really search himself or herself to see if he or she is in the faith:

> Test yourselves *to see* if you are in the faith; examine yourselves! Or do you not recognize this about yourselves, that Jesus Christ is in you—unless indeed you fail the test? (II Corinthians 13:5)

What better time than now to check ourselves to see if we are truly in the faith? What better time to turn to God in prayer, seeking reconciliation?

> Jesus speaking here: "If you then, being evil, know how to give good gifts to your children, how much more will *your* heavenly Father give the Holy Spirit to those who ask Him?" (Luke 11:13)

Made in the USA
Columbia, SC
27 September 2021